Table of Contents

CHAPTER 8

BURGER RECIPES

CHAPTER 9

PASTA RECIPES

INTRODUCTION

Foodies, do you miss going out and dining at your favorite restaurants? Are you craving the delicious steaks from Texas Roadhouse or Caesar salad from the Olive Garden, and crispy bread from Panera? Then wait no further! Here comes a cookbook that will provide you all the copycat recipes from your favorite food outlets in one place. Now you can recreate the authentic Carrabba's flavors and spread the irresistible aromas of cheesecakes from the Cheesecake Factory using this comprehensive collection of recipes. Whether you are a beginner or an expert cook, these recipes will help cook the best out of basic kitchen ingredients. Before jumping straight to the recipes, let's take a quick view of all the restaurants that are covered in this cookbook.

Copycat Meals

Every popular chain in America has its own specialty, like the ice cream from Baskin Robbins has a parallel in its wide variety of flavors. Similarly, the California Pizza Kitchen serves flavorsome pizza, which all have their own signature flavors. And if you miss going to all those places or ordering their specials because of the pandemic, then the copycat recipes are your best shot to cook these delicious meals at home. There is a standard formula that each of these places uses to make a certain meal taste delicious, and the copycat recipes in this cookbook will help you discover all those techniques and formulas. Here you will find the copycat recipes inspired by the following popular American restaurants:

➢ Olive Garden
➢ Cracker Barrel
➢ Applebee's
➢ Arby's
➢ Arthur Treacher's
➢ Bahama Breeze
➢ Baskin-Robbins
➢ Benihana
➢ Boston Market
➢ California Pizza Kitchen

- ➢ Carrabba's Italian Grill
- ➢ Chipotle
- ➢ Taco Bell
- ➢ Chili's
- ➢ P.F Chang's
- ➢ Texas Roadhouse
- ➢ Red Lobster
- ➢ IHOP
- ➢ Panda Express
- ➢ Pei Wei
- ➢ McDonald's
- ➢ Panera Bread
- ➢ Denny's
- ➢ The Cheesecake Factory
- ➢ Starbucks
- ➢ Jamba juice
- ➢ KFC
- ➢ TGI Fridays

The restaurants in the above list are not new to most of us. In fact, we all have grown up going to these places and enjoying their luscious meals. The list covers a wide range of food chains to include all types of cuisines and meal types, including fast food, desserts, bread, Asian cuisines, Italian, steaks, and beverages. So you can pick the best of these recipes and create a special menu of your own!

America's Finest

Here are some of the fun and interesting facts about some of the most popular American food chains covered in this cookbook.

Maggiano's Little Italy

It is an American-based restaurant chain that offers exquisite Italian-American cuisine. There are fewer restaurants in the States that provide authentic Italian flavors in a wide variety of meals, and Maggiano's is one example. The company was officially established in 1991 by Melman's Lettuce Enterprise in Chicago. Initially, two outlets ran at Clark Street and Grand Avenue. Later, in 1995, the concept was extended by Brinker International. By 2015, Maggiano's amazing flavors got a wider outreach through 52 of its new locations in 22 states of America.

Carrabba's Italian Grill

Carrabba is the brainchild of John Charles Johnny Carrabba III. He and his uncle, Damian Mandola, first founded this chain back in 1986. The first-ever restaurant was opened in Houston, Texas, on Kirby Drive. Soon they had to open a second location near Voss Road and Woodway. The restaurant was named after Damian's sister Rosia Carrabba, which was later remembered as Carrabba. The family still owns the original outlets. Due to the rising popularity and demand of Carrabba's food, in 1993, they set out on a joint venture with the predecessors of Bloomin Brands, Outback Steakhouse, and soon the restaurant turned into a national chain.

Olive Garden

The olive garden has made an international name with its fine Italian American cuisine. This is an American restaurant chain that runs under Garden Restaurants, Inc., as a subsidiary. It was first established in Orlando in 1982. As the company grew in size, it established 145 restaurants all over. And soon, with this rate of expansion, the company became the largest Italian chain in the United States. Even in other countries where Olive Garden is not located, people run Olive Garden-inspired food chains; that's how popular it is worldwide.

Texas Roadhouse

Texas Roadhouse is an American chain restaurant specializing in steaks and promoting a Western theme. Texas Roadhouse's headquarters is stationed in Louisville, Kentucky. It is known for its free peanut buckets on each table and free bread rolls. Texas Roadhouse serves American cuisine, including steaks, ribs, chicken, and seafood. The chain holds several culinary championships across the country with ribs and steaks. Everything on the menu is made completely from scratch to order, except for some items from the children's menu. This includes salads, sauce (the only sauce not made from scratch is a low-fat ranch), and side dishes. Each store has its own baker and butcher/meat slicer. Their steaks are hand-cut and never frozen.

Panera Bread

Panera Bread runs more than 2,000 locations; this American bakery/café has earned its name through its unique variety and inspiring flavor. It all began in 1980 when its pioneer first opened a small cookie store in Massachusetts. The company expanded from then onwards, and now it has more than 2,300 bakeries in the USA and Canada. The company is headquartered in Missouri. So, initially, it was all cookies, bread, and basic baked items. But as Panera quickly gained popularity and established its reputation, the creative and skilled team at the bakery expanded the menu and included a variety of other meals to satisfy customers.

Starbucks

Starbucks definitely needs no introduction; this coffeehouse company has gained worldwide popularity through its unique flavors and quality food. Today, Starbucks outlets are operated all around the world. It initially started back in 1971 when the first-ever Starbucks was officially opened. At that time, this coffeehouse offered some of the finest coffees made out of freshly roasted coffee beans. Inspired by the Italian coffee bars, Howard Schultz, the then-chairman of Starbucks, took this experience to the United States and established a coffee house with the aim of providing more than just coffee. And soon, they caught the public eye.

CHAPTER 1

BREAKFAST RECIPES

"Corner Bakery Cafe" Chilled Swiss Oatmeal

Ingredients

- ➢ 2 cups old-fashioned oats
- ➢ 1 ¾ cups skim milk
- ➢ 1 cup plain Greek yogurt

- ➤ 1 apple, cored and cut into small pieces
- ➤ 1 banana, peeled and cut into small pieces
- ➤ 4 tablespoons dried cranberries
- ➤ 1 teaspoon vanilla extract
- ➤ 1/8 teaspoon ground cinnamon
- ➤ Pinch of salt
- ➤ ¼ cup almonds, toasted and sliced

How to Prepare

1. In a bowl, add all ingredients (except for almonds) and gently stir to combine.
2. Cover the bowl and place in the refrigerator overnight.
3. In the morning, remove the bowl from the refrigerator and gently stir the oatmeal.
4. Serve with the almond topping.

Preparation time: 10 minutes
Total time: 10 minutes
Servings: 6

Nutritional Values

- ➤ *Calories 220*
- ➤ *Total Fat 4.4 g*
- ➤ *Saturated Fat 0.9 g*
- ➤ *Cholesterol 4 mg*
- ➤ *Sodium 96 mg*
- ➤ *Total Carbs 5.4 g*
- ➤ *Fiber 4.8 g*
- ➤ *Sugar 13.4 g*
- ➤ *Protein 9.8 g*

"Burger King" French Toast Sticks

Ingredients

- ➢ 6 day-old Texas toast slices
- ➢ 4 large eggs
- ➢ 1 cup 2% milk
- ➢ 2 tablespoons sugar
- ➢ 1 teaspoon vanilla extract
- ➢ ¼–½ teaspoon ground cinnamon
- ➢ 1 cup cornflakes, crushed

➢ 1 tablespoon confectioners' sugar
➢ 1/3 cup maple syrup

How to Prepare

1. Cut each bread slice into thirds.
2. Arrange the breadsticks into an ungreased 13 x 9-inch baking dish in a single layer.
3. In a large bowl, add eggs, milk, sugar, vanilla extract, and cinnamon, and beat until well combined.
4. Place the egg mixture over breadsticks evenly and set aside for about 2 minutes, turning once.
5. Now, coat breadsticks with cornflake crumbs evenly.
6. Arrange the breadsticks in a greased 15 x 10 x 1-inch baking dish for about 45 minutes and freeze until firm.
7. Preheat the oven to 425°F.
8. Arrange the breadsticks onto a greased baking sheet in a single layer and bake for about 8 minutes.
9. Flip the breadsticks and bake for about 10–12 minutes or until golden-brown.
10. Remove the baking sheet from oven and transfer the breadsticks onto a platter.
11. Sprinkle with confectioners' sugar and serve with the drizzling of maple syrup.

Preparation time: 15 minutes
Cooking time: 20 minutes
Total time: 35 minutes
Servings: 6

Nutritional Values

➢ *Calories 184*
➢ *Total Fat 4.6 g*
➢ *Saturated Fat 1.5 g*
➢ *Cholesterol 127 mg*

> *Sodium 176 mg*
> *Total Carbs 28.8 g*
> *Fiber 0.6 g*
> *Sugar 18.9 g*
> *Protein 6.7 g*

"McDonald's" Egg McMuffin

Ingredients

- ➢ 4 cups biscuit/baking mix
- ➢ 2 cups cheddar cheese, shredded and divided
- ➢ 1 cup cooked ham, chopped finely
- ➢ 1 ¼ teaspoons ground black pepper, divided
- ➢ 1 ½ cups 2% milk, divided
- ➢ 3 tablespoons butter, melted
- ➢ 8 large eggs

➢   1/8 teaspoon salt

➢   2 tablespoons butter

How to Prepare

1. Preheat the oven to 425°F.
2. In a large bowl, add biscuit mix, 1 cup of cheese, ham, and ½ teaspoon of black pepper, and mix well.
3. Add 1 cup of milk and mix just until just combined.
4. Place the dough onto a lightly floured surface and with your hands, gently knead 8–10 times.
5. Now, roll the dough into 1-inch thickness.
6. With a floured 2½-inch biscuit cutter, cut into biscuits.
7. Arrange the biscuits onto an ungreased baking sheet about 2 inches apart.
8. Brush each biscuit with melted butter and sprinkle with ½ teaspoon of black pepper.
9. Bake for about 12–14 minutes or until golden-brown.
10. Meanwhile, in a bowl, add eggs, remaining milk, salt, and remaining black pepper, and beat until well combined.
11. In a large non-stick skillet, melt butter over medium heat.
12. Add the egg mixture and cook until all the liquid is absorbed and eggs are thickened.
13. Stir in the remaining cheddar cheese and remove from heat.
14. Remove the biscuits from heat and set aside to cool slightly.
15. Carefully split the warm biscuits in half.
16. Place the egg mixture over bottom half of each biscuit.
17. Cover with top halves and serve.

Preparation time: 15 minutes
Cooking time: 14 minutes
Total time: 29 minutes
Servings: 10

Nutritional Values

- ➤ *Calories 45*
- ➤ *Total Fat 26.2 g*
- ➤ *Saturated Fat 12.3 g*
- ➤ *Cholesterol 199 mg*
- ➤ *Sodium 1,000 mg*
- ➤ *Total Carbs 32 g*
- ➤ *Fiber 1.2 g*
- ➤ *Sugar 7.4 g*
- ➤ *Protein 17.8 g*

"Dunkin Donuts" Power Breakfast Sandwich

Ingredients

- ➢ 6 large eggs
- ➢ ¼ cup onion, chopped
- ➢ ¼ cup red bell pepper, seeded and chopped
- ➢ ¼ cup fresh baby spinach, chopped
- ➢ ¼ teaspoon salt

- ➤ ½ teaspoon ground black pepper
- ➤ 6 sweet Italian turkey sausage links, casing removed
- ➤ 6 multigrain sandwich thins
- ➤ 6 Pepper Jack cheese slices

How to Prepare

1. Preheat the oven to 350°F.
2. Grease 6 cups of a muffin tin.
3. Heat a lightly greased skillet over medium heat and sauté onion and bell peppers for about 5 minutes.
4. Stir in spinach and remove from the heat.
5. Set aside to cool slightly.
6. In a bowl, add eggs, spinach mixture, salt, and black pepper, and beat until well combined.
7. Divide the egg mixture into prepared muffin cups evenly.
8. Bake for about 13–15 minutes or until eggs are done completely.
9. Meanwhile, shape each sausage link into a patty.
10. Heat a greased skillet over medium heat and cook the sausage patties for about 3–4 minutes or until cooked through.
11. Transfer the patties onto a paper towel-lined plate and set aside.
12. Remove the muffin tin from oven and set aside for about 5 minutes.
13. Carefully remove the egg bites from muffin tin.
14. Arrange the bottom halves of sandwich thins onto each serving plate.
15. Top each with 1 sausage patty, followed by egg bite add a cheese slice.
16. Cover with the other half of the sandwich thin and serve.

Preparation time: 15 minutes
Cooking time: 15 minutes
Total time: 30 minutes
Servings: 6

Nutritional Values

- Calories 557
- Total Fat 36.6 g
- Saturated Fat 14.2 g
- Cholesterol 277 mg
- Sodium 1,202 mg
- Total Carbs 2.9 g
- Fiber 5.3 g
- Sugar 1.9 g
- Protein 32. g

"Waffle House" Pecan Waffles

Ingredients

- 1 ½ cups all-purpose flour
- ½ teaspoon baking powder
- ¼ teaspoon salt
- 1 ¼ cups milk
- 1 egg
- ½ cup granulated sugar
- 4 tablespoons butter, melted and cooled

➢   1 teaspoon vanilla extract
➢   1 cup pecans, chopped
➢   ½ cup maple syrup

How to Prepare

1. In a large bowl, add flour, baking soda, and salt, and mix well.
2. In another bowl, add egg, sugar, butter, and vanilla extract, and beat until smooth.
3. Add the flour mixture and mix until just combined.
4. Gently fold in 1/3 cup of the pecans.
5. Preheat the waffle iron and then grease it.
6. Add ¼ of the mixture in preheated waffle iron and cook for about 3–4 minutes.
7. Repeat with the remaining mixture.
8. Serve warm with the topping of maple syrup and remaining pecans.

Preparation time: 15 minutes
Cooking time: 16 minutes
Total time: 31 minutes
Servings: 4

Nutritional Values

➢   *Calories 68*
➢   *Total Fat 36.6 g*
➢   *Saturated Fat 10.8 g*
➢   *Cholesterol 78 mg*
➢   *Sodium 285 mg*
➢   *Total Carbs 83.2 g*
➢   *Fiber 4.4 g*
➢   *Sugar 54.2 g*
➢   *Protein 10.4 g*

"Starbucks" Pumpkin Bread

Ingredients

- ➢ ¾ cup white whole-wheat flour
- ➢ ¾ cup all-purpose flour
- ➢ 1 teaspoon baking soda
- ➢ ½ teaspoon baking powder
- ➢ 1 ¾ teaspoon pumpkin pie spice
- ➢ ½ teaspoon salt
- ➢ 1 cup pumpkin puree
- ➢ ½ cup pure maple syrup
- ➢ 1/3 cup granulated sugar

- ➢ 2 egg whites
- ➢ ¼ cup coconut oil, melted
- ➢ ¼ cup water
- ➢ ¼ cup pepitas, toasted

How to Prepare

1. Preheat oven to 350°F.
2. Grease a 9 ½ x 5-inch loaf pan.
3. In a large bowl, add flours, baking soda, baking powder, pumpkin pie spice, and salt, and mix well.
4. In another bowl, add remaining ingredients (except for pepitas) and beat until well combined.
5. Add flour mixture and mix until just combined.
6. Place the mixture into the prepared loaf pan evenly and sprinkle with pepitas.
7. Bake for about 40 minutes or until a toothpick inserted in the center comes out clean.
8. Remove the loaf pan from oven and place onto a wire rack to cool for about 10 minutes.
9. Carefully invert the bread onto the wire rack to cool completely before serving.
10. With a sharp knife, cut the bread into desired-sized slices and serve.

Preparation time: 15 minutes
Cooking time: 40 minutes
Total time: 55 minutes
Servings: 12

Nutritional Values

- ➢ *Calories 178*
- ➢ *Total Fat 6.2 g*
- ➢ *Saturated Fat 4. g*
- ➢ *Cholesterol 0 mg*

> *Sodium 210 mg*
> *Total Carbs 28.8 g*
> *Fiber 1.2 g*
> *Sugar 14.2 g*
> *Protein .2 g*

"Denny's" Ham and Cheese Omelet

Ingredients

- ➤ 3 eggs
- ➤ 3 tablespoons water
- ➤ 1/8 teaspoon salt
- ➤ 1/8 teaspoon ground black pepper
- ➤ 1 tablespoon butter
- ➤ ½ cup fully-cooked ham, cubed
- ➤ ¼ cup Swiss cheese, shredded

How to Prepare

1. In a bowl, add the eggs, water, salt, and black pepper, and beat until well combined.
2. In a small non-stick skillet, melt butter over medium-high heat.
3. Add the egg mixture into the skillet and cook for about 1–2 minutes or until set.
4. With a spoon, push cooked edges toward the center, letting the uncooked portion flow underneath.
5. Place ham on one side of egg mixture and sprinkle with cheese.
6. Fold the other side over the filling and transfer the omelet onto a plate.
7. Serve hot.

Preparation time: 10 minutes
Cooking time: 5 minutes
Total time: 15 minutes
Servings: 2

Nutritional Values

- *Calories 252*
- *Total Fat 19 g*
- *Saturated Fat 9.1 g*
- *Cholesterol 292 mg*
- *Sodium 747 mg*
- *Total Carbs 2.6 g*
- *Fiber 0.5 g*
- *Sugar 0.7 g*
- *Protein 17.6 g*

"Starbucks" Egg Bites

Ingredients

- ➢ ½ cup Monterey Jack cheese, shredded
- ➢ ½ cup cottage cheese
- ➢ 4 eggs
- ➢ ¼ teaspoon salt
- ➢ ¼ teaspoon ground black pepper

➢ ¼ cup roasted red pepper, chopped
➢ ¼ cup fresh spinach, chopped
➢ 1 scallion, chopped
➢ ¼ teaspoon hot sauce

How to Prepare

1. In a bowl, add the cheeses, eggs, salt, and black pepper, and with an immersion blender, blend until smooth.
2. Add the red pepper, spinach, scallion, and hot sauce, and stir to combine.
3. Divide the mixture into the silicone egg cups evenly.
4. With 1 foil piece, cover each cup.
5. Arrange the trivet in the bottom of an Instant Pot and pour 1 cup of water.
6. Place the molds on top of trivet in a single layer.
7. Secure the lid and place the pressure valve to *Seal* position.
8. Select *Steam* and just use the default time of 10 minutes.
9. Select *Cancel* and do a *Natural* release for about 10 minutes. Then do a "Quick" release.
10. Remove the lid and place the molds onto a wire rack for about 2–4 minutes.
11. Carefully remove the foil and serve.

Preparation time: 15 minutes
Cooking time: 10 minutes
Total time: 25 minutes
Servings: 3

Nutritional Values
➢ *Calories 195*
➢ *Total Fat 12.3 g*
➢ *Saturated Fat 5.9 g*
➢ *Cholesterol 28 mg*

> *Sodium 580 mg*
> *Total Carbs 3.5g*
> *Fiber 0.4 g*
> *Sugar 1.5 g*
> *Protein 17.5 g*

"Coco's Bakery" Santa Fe Quiche

Ingredients

- ➢ 1 (9-inch) unbaked pastry shell
- ➢ 1 teaspoon red chili powder
- ➢ 1 cup Monterey Jack cheese, shredded
- ➢ 1 cup cheddar cheese, shredded
- ➢ 1 tablespoon all-purpose flour
- ➢ 1 ½ cups half-and-half
- ➢ 3 large eggs, beaten

➢ 1 (4-ounce) can chopped green chiles, drained
➢ 1 (2 ¼-ounce) can sliced ripe olives, drained
➢ Salt and ground black pepper, as required

How to Prepare:

1. Preheat the oven to 325ºF.
2. Arrange the crust over a lightly greased pie plate and sprinkle the inside with chili powder.
3. In a bowl, add the cheeses and flour and mix well.
4. In another bowl, add half-and-half, eggs, chiles, olives, salt, and black pepper, and beat until well combined.
5. Place the cheese mixture over the crust evenly and top with egg mixture.
6. Bake for about 45–55 minutes or until a wooden skewer inserted in the center comes out clean.
7. Remove the pie plate from oven and place onto a wire rack to cool for about 10 minutes before cutting.
8. Cut into desired-sized wedges and serve.

Preparation time: 15 minutes
Cooking time: 55 minutes
Total time: 1 hour, 10 minutes
Servings: 6

Nutritional Values

➢ *Calories 377*
➢ *Total Fat 29 g*
➢ *Saturated Fat 14.4 g*
➢ *Cholesterol 152 mg*
➢ *Sodium 519 mg*
➢ *Total Carbs 1.8 g*
➢ *Fiber 0.8 g*
➢ *Sugar 1.3 g*
➢ *Protein 15.7 g*

"IHOP" Buttermilk Pancakes

Ingredients

- 1 ¼ cups all-purpose flour
- 2 ½ teaspoon sugar
- 1 ½ teaspoons baking powder
- ½ teaspoon baking soda
- ½ teaspoon salt
- 1 egg, beaten
- 1 ½ cups buttermilk
- 2 tablespoons vegetable oil

➢ ¼ cup maple syrup

How to Prepare

1. In a bowl, add flour, sugar, baking powder, baking soda, sugar, and salt, and mix well.
2. Add the egg, buttermilk, and oil, and beat until smooth.
3. Heat a lightly greased skillet over medium-low heat.
4. Add ¼ of the mixture and spread in an even circle.
5. Cook for about 2 minutes or until golden-brown.
6. Flip and cook for about 1–2 minutes or until golden-brown.
7. Repeat with the remaining mixture.
8. Serve warm with the drizzling of maple syrup.

Preparation time: 15 minutes
Cooking time: 16 minutes
Total time: 10 minutes
Servings: 4

Nutritional Values
➢ *Calories 317*
➢ *Total Fat 9.1 g*
➢ *Saturated Fat 2.2 g*
➢ *Cholesterol 45 mg*
➢ *Sodium 565 mg*
➢ *Total Carbs 50.9 g*
➢ *Fiber 1.1 g*
➢ *Sugar 18.8 g*
➢ *Protein 8.5 g*

CHAPTER 2
SNACK & SIDE RECIPES

"Applebee's" Queso Blanco

Ingredients
- ➢ 2 tablespoons vegetable oil
- ➢ 1/3 cup white onion, chopped finely
- ➢ 2 tablespoons jalapeño pepper, minced finely
- ➢ 1 pound white American cheese, cut into large pieces
- ➢ 8 ounces Monterey Jack cheese, cut into large pieces

> ½ cup half-and-half
> 1/3–½ cup tomato, chopped
> 2 tablespoons fresh cilantro, chopped and divided
> 1 jalapeño pepper, chopped

How to Prepare

1. In a medium pan, heat oil over medium-low heat and sauté onion and minced jalapeño pepper for about 2–3 minutes.
2. Add cheeses and half-and-half and stir to combine.
3. Reduce the heat to low and cook for about 2–3 minutes, or until cheeses are melted.
4. Add the tomato pieces and stir to combine.
5. Stir in half of the cilantro and remove from the heat.
6. Serve with the garnishing with remaining cilantro and chopped jalapeno.

Preparation time: 15 minutes
Cooking time: 8 minutes
Total time: 23 minutes
Servings: 10

Nutritional Values
> *Calories 306*
> *Total Fat 25.6 g*
> *Saturated Fat 13.8 g*
> *Cholesterol 65 mg*
> *Sodium 807 mg*
> *Total Carbs 4.6 g*
> *Fiber 0.2 g*
> *Sugar 3.7 g*
> *Protein 14.1 g*

"Olive Garden" Stuffed Mushrooms

Ingredients

- ➢ 6 ounces clams
- ➢ 1 tablespoon butter, softened
- ➢ 1 tablespoon scallion, chopped finely
- ➢ ½ teaspoon garlic, minced
- ➢ 1 teaspoon dried oregano
- ➢ 1/8 teaspoon garlic salt
- ➢ ½ cup Italian breadcrumbs

➤ 1 egg, beaten
➤ ¼ cup plus 2 tablespoons mozzarella cheese, grated and divided
➤ 2 tablespoons Parmesan cheese, grated
➤ 1 tablespoon Romano cheese, grated
➤ ¼ cup butter, melted
➤ 8 mushrooms, stems removed
➤ 2 tablespoons fresh parsley, chopped

How to Prepare

1. Preheat the oven to 350°F.
2. Grease a baking dish.
3. Drain the clams, reserving the liquid in a bowl.
4. In a bowl, add the clams, softened butter, scallion, garlic, oregano, and garlic salt, and mix well.
5. Add the reserved clam juice, breadcrumbs, and egg, and mix until well combined.
6. Add 2 tablespoons of mozzarella, Parmesan, and Romano cheese, and mix well.
7. Arrange the mushrooms onto a platter and stuff the cavity of each with clam mixture.
8. Arrange the mushrooms into the prepared baking dish and drizzle with melted butter.
9. Bake for about 35–40 minutes.
10. Remove from the oven and sprinkle the mushrooms with remaining mozzarella cheese.
11. Bake for about 5 minutes or until the cheese is just slightly melted.
12. Remove from the oven and place the mushrooms onto a platter.
13. Garnish with parsley and serve.

Preparation time: 20 minutes
Cooking time: 45 minutes
Total time: 10 minutes
Servings: 4

Nutritional Values

- Calories 282
- Total Fat 19.9 g
- Saturated Fat 11.7 g
- Cholesterol 90 mg
- Sodium 495 mg
- Total Carbs 16.89 g
- Fiber 1.4 g
- Sugar 3.1 g
- Protein 10.4 g

"Red Lobster" Cheddar Bay Biscuits

Ingredients

- ➢ 2 cups Bisquick baking mix
- ➢ ¾ cup sharp cheddar cheese, shredded
- ➢ ½ cup cold water
- ➢ 4 tablespoons butter
- ➢ 1 teaspoon dried parsley flakes
- ➢ ½ teaspoon dried Italian seasoning

> ½ teaspoon garlic powder

How to Prepare

1. Preheat the oven to 350°F.
2. In a bowl, add Bisquick, cheddar cheese, and water, and mix until well combined.
3. Place the dough onto a lightly floured surface and roll into ¾-inch thickness.
4. With a biscuit cutter, cut the biscuits and arrange onto a baking sheet.
5. Bake for about 8–10 minutes or until the tops are golden-brown.
6. Meanwhile, in a small pan, add butter, parsley, Italian seasoning, and garlic powder, and cook until butter is melted completely, stirring continuously.
7. Remove the biscuits from oven and brush each with the butter mixture.
8. Serve immediately.

Preparation time: 15 minutes
Cooking time: 10 minutes
Total time: 25 minutes
Servings: 8

Nutritional Values

> *Calories 217*
> *Total Fat 13.8 g*
> *Saturated Fat 7 g*
> *Cholesterol 27 mg*
> *Sodium 471 mg*
> *Total Carbs 18.4 g*
> *Fiber 0.6 g*
> *Sugar 3.5 g*
> *Protein 5 g*

"The Cheesecake Factory" Nashville Hot Chicken Nuggets

Ingredients

Nuggets

- ➢ 6 chicken breasts, cut into nugget-sized chunks
- ➢ 4 cups pickle juice

- ➤ 3 cups all-purpose flour
- ➤ 1 tablespoon cayenne pepper
- ➤ 1 teaspoon paprika
- ➤ 1 teaspoon garlic powder
- ➤ Salt and ground black pepper, to taste
- ➤ 2 eggs
- ➤ 1 cup whole milk
- ➤ 1 ½ tablespoons Louisiana hot sauce
- ➤ 2 cups vegetable oil
- ➤ ½ cup pickle slices

<u>Nashville Sauce</u>

- ➤ ¾ cups butter, melted
- ➤ 1 tablespoon dark brown sugar
- ➤ 1 tablespoon honey
- ➤ 1 tablespoon Louisiana hot sauce
- ➤ 2 tablespoons cayenne pepper
- ➤ 1 teaspoon paprika
- ➤ 2/3 teaspoons garlic powder
- ➤ Salt and ground black pepper, to taste

How to Prepare

1. In a large bowl, add the chicken chunks and pickle juice and coat well.
2. Cover the bowl tightly and refrigerate overnight.
3. In a shallow bowl, add the flour, spices, salt, and black pepper, and mix well.
4. In a separate shallow bowl, add eggs, milk, and hot sauce, and beat until well combined.
5. Remove chicken chunks from brine and, with paper towels, pat them dry.
6. Coat the chicken chunks with the flour and then dip into egg mixture.
7. In a large heavy-bottomed pan, heat the oil over medium heat and cook the nuggets in 3 batches for about 6–8 minutes or until light

golden-brown.

8. With a slotted spoon, transfer the nuggets onto a paper towel-lined plate.

9. Let them rest for about 1 minute.

10. Return the nuggets into the oil and cook for about 2 minutes more.

11. With a slotted spoon, transfer the nuggets onto a paper towel-lined plate.

12. **Nashville Sauce:** In a small bowl, add all ingredients and mix well until combined.

13. Brush the warm nuggets with sauce and serve alongside the pickle slices.

Preparation time: 20 minutes
Cooking time: 30 minutes
Total time: 50 minutes
Servings: 8

Nutritional Values

- *Calories 970*
- *Total Fat 77.2 g*
- *Saturated Fat 22.8 g*
- *Cholesterol 172 mg*
- *Sodium 448 mg*
- *Total Carbs 44.6 g*
- *Fiber 3.2 g*
- *Sugar 16.4 g*
- *Protein 26.2 g*

"The Cheesecake Factory" Loaded Baked Potato Tots

Ingredients

- ➢ 2 cups mashed potatoes
- ➢ 3–4 cooked bacon strips, crumbled
- ➢ 1 cup sharp cheddar cheese

- ➤ ½ cup sour cream
- ➤ ¼ cup milk
- ➤ 2 tablespoons fresh chives, minced
- ➤ 2 eggs
- ➤ 1 cup panko breadcrumbs
- ➤ 1–2 cups oil

How to Prepare

1. In a bowl, add mashed potatoes, bacon, cheese, sour cream, milk, and chives, and mix until well combined.
2. Make about 1-inch balls from mixture.
3. In a shallow dish, crack eggs and beat well.
4. In another shallow bowl, place the breadcrumbs.
5. Dip the potato balls in beaten egg and then coat with breadcrumbs.
6. Arrange the balls onto a parchment paper-lined baking sheet and refrigerate for about 5–10 minutes.
7. In a deep pan, heat the oil over medium heat and fry the balls in 3 batches for about 3–4 minutes or until golden-brown.
8. With a slotted spoon, transfer balls onto a paper towel-lined plate to drain.
9. Serve warm.

Preparation time: 15 minutes
Cooking time: 12 minutes
Total time: 27 minutes
Servings: 8

Nutritional Values

- ➤ *Calories 482*
- ➤ *Total Fat 41.7 g*
- ➤ *Saturated Fat 10.7 g*
- ➤ *Cholesterol 75 mg*
- ➤ *Sodium 368 mg*
- ➤ *Total Carbs 9.4 g*

- *Fiber 1 g*
- *Sugar 1 g*
- *Protein 10.6 g*

"Boston Market" Creamed Spinach

Ingredients

<u>White Sauce</u>

- ➢ 3 tablespoons butter
- ➢ 4 tablespoons flour
- ➢ ¼ teaspoon salt
- ➢ 1 cup whole milk

<u>Spinach</u>

- ➢ 20 ounces frozen chopped spinach, thawed and drained
- ➢ ½ cup sour cream

- ➢ 1 teaspoon salt
- ➢ 2 tablespoon butter
- ➢ 2 tablespoons onion, chopped
- ➢ ¼ cup water

How to Prepare

1. **White sauce:** In a pan, melt butter over medium-low heat.
2. Add flour and salt and stir until well combined and smooth.
3. Slowly, add milk, beating continuously until mixture becomes thick and smooth.
4. Place butter in a 2-quart saucepan on medium heat, add onions.
5. Meanwhile, for spinach: in a non-stick skillet, melt butter over medium heat and sauté the onion for about 4–5 minutes.
6. Add the spinach, water, and salt, and stir to combine.
7. Reduce the heat to low and simmer, covered for about 3–4 minutes, stirring occasionally.
8. Add white sauce and sour cream and cook for about 1–2 minutes, stirring continuously.
9. Serve hot.

Preparation time: 15 minutes
Cooking time: 15 minutes
Total time: 10 minutes
Servings: 6

Nutritional Values

- ➢ *Calories 192*
- ➢ *Total Fat 15.4 g*
- ➢ *Saturated Fat 9.4 g*
- ➢ *Cholesterol 38 mg*
- ➢ *Sodium 557 mg*
- ➢ *Total Carbs 10.4 g*
- ➢ *Fiber 2.3 g*
- ➢ *Sugar 2.7 g*

➤ *Protein 5.3 g*

"The Cheesecake Factory" Garlic Mashed Potatoes

Ingredients

- ➢ ¼ cup whole garlic cloves
- ➢ 1 tablespoon olive oil
- ➢ 2 pounds red potatoes, cut in half
- ➢ ½ cup milk

- ➢ ¼ cup heavy cream
- ➢ 2 tablespoons butter
- ➢ Salt and ground black pepper, to taste

How to Prepare

1. Preheat the oven to 400°F.
2. Coat the garlic cloves with oil evenly.
3. Place the garlic cloves onto a piece of foil in a single layer.
4. Wrap the garlic cloves tightly.
5. Roast for about 45 minutes or until soft.
6. Remove from the oven and unwrap the garlic cloves. Set aside to cool.
7. In a large pan of water, add the potatoes over medium-high heat and bring to a boil.
8. Cook for about 20–30 minutes or until tender.
9. Drain the potatoes and transfer into a large bowl.
10. With a potato masher, mash the potatoes slightly.
11. Add the remaining ingredients and mash until mostly creamy.
12. Serve warm.

Preparation time: 15 minutes
Cooking time: 1 hour, 35 minutes
Total time: 10 minutes
Servings: 4

Nutritional Values

- ➢ *Calories 293*
- ➢ *Total Fat 13 g*
- ➢ *Saturated Fat 6.4 g*
- ➢ *Cholesterol 28 mg*
- ➢ *Sodium 112 mg*
- ➢ *Total Carbs 40.6 g*
- ➢ *Fiber 4 g*

- *Sugar .7 g*
- *Protein 6 g*

"Cracker Barrel" Fried Apples

Ingredients

- 4 tablespoons butter
- 6 tart apples; peeled, cored, and sliced
- 1 teaspoon fresh lemon juice
- ¼ cup brown sugar
- 1/8 teaspoon salt
- 1 teaspoon ground cinnamon
- Pinch of ground nutmeg

How to Prepare

1. In a large non-stick skillet, melt butter over medium heat.
2. Arrange the apple slices over butter evenly and drizzle with lemon juice.
3. Now, sprinkle with brown sugar and salt.
4. Arrange the heat to low and cook, covered for about 15 minutes.
5. Remove from the heat and sprinkle with cinnamon and nutmeg.
6. Serve warm.

Preparation time: 10 minutes
Cooking time: 15 minutes
Total time: 25 minutes
Servings: 8

Nutritional Values

- *Calories 156*
- *Total Fat 6.1 g*
- *Saturated Fat 3.7 g*
- *Cholesterol 15 mg*
- *Sodium 79 mg*
- *Total Carbs 27.8 g*
- *Fiber 4.2 g*
- *Sugar 21.8 g*
- *Protein 0.5 g*

"The Cheesecake Factory" Crispy Brussels Sprouts

Ingredients

➢ 1 ½ pounds Brussels sprouts, trimmed
➢ 1/3 cup unsalted butter
➢ 3 tablespoons pure maple syrup

- ➢ 1–2 cups canola oil
- ➢ Salt, to taste
- ➢ 4 cooked bacon slices, chopped

How to Prepare

1. Remove the outer leaves of Brussels sprouts to equal 1 ½ cups. Set aside.
2. Cut the remaining sprout cores into quarters.
3. In a small saucepan, add butter and maple syrup over medium heat and bring to a gentle simmer, stirring frequently.
4. Remove from the heat and set aside to cool slightly.
5. In a large saucepan, heat the oil over medium-high heat and fry sprout cores in 3 batches for about 1–2 minutes or until slightly crispy.
6. With a slotted spoon, transfer the sprout cores onto a paper towel-lined plate to drain.
7. Sprinkle the sprout cores with ½ teaspoon salt.
8. In the same pan of oil, add sprout leaves in 2 batches and fry for about 30 seconds or until slightly crispy.
9. With a slotted spoon, transfer the sprout leaves onto a paper towels-lined plate to drain.
10. Sprinkle the sprout leaves with the remaining salt.
11. Transfer sprout cores and leaves into a bowl.
12. Add bacon and warm maple mixture and toss to coat.
13. Serve immediately.

Preparation time: 15 minutes
Cooking time: 10 minutes
Total time: 25 minutes
Servings: 4

Nutritional Values
- ➢ *Calories 885*

- ➢ *Total Fat 84.1 g*
- ➢ *Saturated Fat 17.9 g*
- ➢ *Cholesterol 73 mg*
- ➢ *Sodium 862 mg*
- ➢ *Total Carbs 25.9 g*
- ➢ *Fiber 6.4 g*
- ➢ *Sugar 12.6 g*
- ➢ *Protein 16.7 g*

"Captain D's" Coleslaw

Ingredients

- ➤ 2 pounds cabbage, chopped finely
- ➤ ¼ pound carrots, peeled and chopped finely
- ➤ 2 tablespoons white onion, chopped finely
- ➤ ¾ cup mayonnaise
- ➤ 2 tablespoons white distilled vinegar
- ➤ 2 teaspoons sugar
- ➤ ½ teaspoon celery seed
- ➤ Salt, to taste

How to Prepare

1. In a large serving bowl, place cabbage, celery, and onions.
2. In a small bowl, add mayonnaise, vinegar, sugar, celery seed, and salt, and beat until well combined.
3. Place dressing over salad and gently, stir to combine.
4. Cover the bowl and refrigerate for at least 2 hours before serving.

Preparation time: 10 minutes
Cooking time: 30 minutes
Total time: 10 minutes
Servings: 8

Nutritional Values
- *Calories 126*
- *Total Fat 7.5 g*
- *Saturated Fat 1.1 g*
- *Cholesterol 6 mg*
- *Sodium 206 mg*
- *Total Carbs 14.5 g*
- *Fiber 3.3 g*
- *Sugar 6.9 g*
- *Protein 1.8 g*

CHAPTER 3
SOUP RECIPES

"Chinese Imperial Place" Egg Drop Soup

Ingredients

- 1 egg
- 2 teaspoons sesame oil, toasted and divided

- ➢ 6 cups chicken broth
- ➢ Salt, to taste
- ➢ ¼ teaspoon ground white pepper
- ➢ 3 scallion greens, sliced

How to Prepare

1. In a small bowl, add the egg and 1 teaspoon of sesame oil and beat slightly. Set aside.
2. In a pan, add the broth over medium-low heat and bring to a boil.
3. Slowly add in the egg mixture, stirring continuously with a fork.
4. Add the remaining sesame oil, salt, and white pepper, and stir to combine.
5. Simmer for about 4–5 minutes or until desired thickness of soup, stirring continuously
6. Serve hot with the garnishing of scallion.

Preparation time: 10 minutes
Cooking time: 10 minutes
Total time: 20 minutes
Servings: 6

Nutritional Values

- ➢ *Calories 65*
- ➢ *Total Fat 3.6 g*
- ➢ *Saturated Fat 0.8 g*
- ➢ *Cholesterol 27 mg*
- ➢ *Sodium 802 mg*
- ➢ *Total Carbs 1.6 g*
- ➢ *Fiber 0.2 g*
- ➢ *Sugar 0.9 g*
- ➢ *Protein 5.9 g*

"Applebee's" Tomato Basil Soup

Ingredients

- ➢ 3 tablespoons olive oil
- ➢ 1 small garlic clove, minced
- ➢ 1 (10 ¾-ounce) can condensed tomato soup
- ➢ ¼ cup bottled marinara sauce
- ➢ ½ of (10 ¾-ounce) can water
- ➢ 1 teaspoon fresh oregano, chopped
- ➢ ½ teaspoon ground black pepper

- ➢ 1 tablespoon fresh basil, chopped
- ➢ 6 Italian-style seasoned croutons
- ➢ 2 tablespoons Parmesan cheese, grated

How to Prepare

1. In a large saucepan, heat the olive oil over medium heat and sauté the garlic for about 2 minutes.
2. Add the condensed tomato soup and marinara sauce and stir to combine.
3. Slowly add the water, stirring continuously.
4. Stir in the oregano and black pepper and bring to a gentle boil.
5. Reduce the heat to low and cook for about 15 minutes.
6. Stir in the basil and remove from the heat.
7. Serve hot with the topping of croutons and Parmesan cheese.

Preparation time: 10 minutes
Cooking time: 20 minutes
Total time: 30 minutes
Servings: 2

Nutritional Values

- ➢ *Calories 411*
- ➢ *Total Fat 27 g*
- ➢ *Saturated Fat 4.1 g*
- ➢ *Cholesterol 5 mg*
- ➢ *Sodium 1,100 mg*
- ➢ *Total Carbs 40.6 g*
- ➢ *Fiber 4.6 g*
- ➢ *Sugar 15.2 g*
- ➢ *Protein 5.2 g*

"Panera Bread" Broccoli Cheddar Soup

Ingredients

- ➢ 2 tablespoons butter
- ➢ ½ cup white onions, chopped
- ➢ 2 tablespoons all-purpose flour
- ➢ 1 cup half-and-half
- ➢ 16 ounces frozen broccoli, chopped
- ➢ 16 ounces American cheese
- ➢ 29 ounces low-sodium chicken broth
- ➢ 1 cup carrots, shredded

- ➢ 8 ounces cheddar cheese, shredded
- ➢ Salt and ground black pepper, to taste

How to Prepare

1. In a large soup pan, melt the butter over medium heat.
2. Stir in the onion and flour and cook for about 1 minute, stirring continuously.
3. Slowly, add the half-and-half, beating continuously until thickened and smooth.
4. Add the broccoli and American cheese and cook for about 2–3 minutes, or until cheese is completely melted.
5. Add the chicken broth, 1 cup at a time, stirring occasionally until well combined.
6. Stir in the carrots and simmer for about 10 minutes.
7. Stir in the cheddar cheese and simmer for about 10 minutes.
8. Season with salt and black pepper and serve hot.

Preparation time: 15 minutes
Cooking time: 30 minutes
Total time: 45 minutes
Servings: 6

Nutritional Values

- ➢ *Calories 543*
- ➢ *Total Fat 40.3 g*
- ➢ *Saturated Fat 24.6 g*
- ➢ *Cholesterol 125 mg*
- ➢ *Sodium 1,300 mg*
- ➢ *Total Carbs 18.4 g*
- ➢ *Fiber 2.7 g*
- ➢ *Sugar 8.5 g*
- ➢ *Protein 28.3 g*

"Outback Steakhouse" Walkabout Soup

Ingredients

Soup

➢ 2 cups sweet onions, sliced thinly

- ➤ 3 tablespoon butter
- ➤ 14 ½ ounces chicken broth
- ➤ Salt and ground black pepper, to taste
- ➤ 2 chicken bouillon cubes
- ➤ ¼ cup Velveeta cheese

White Sauce
- ➤ 3 tablespoons butter
- ➤ 3 tablespoons flour
- ➤ ¼ teaspoon salt
- ➤ 1 ½ cups whole milk

How to Prepare

1. **Soup:** In a large soup pan, place butter and onion over medium-low heat and cook for about 8–10 minutes, stirring frequently.
2. Add broth, bouillon cubes, salt, and black pepper, and cook for about 3–4 minutes.
3. **White sauce:** In a large pan, melt butter over medium heat.
4. Add the flour and cook until thickened, stirring continuously.
5. Slowly add milk, beating continuously until smooth and thick.
6. Stir in salt and remove from heat.
7. In the pan of soup, add white sauce and Velveeta cheese and stir to combine.
8. Reduce the heat to medium-low and cook for about 2–3 minutes, stirring continuously.
9. Now, reduce the heat to low and simmer for about 30–45 minutes.
10. Serve hot.

Preparation time: 15 minutes
Cooking time: 1 hour, 5 minutes
Total time: 1 hour, 20 minutes
Servings: 4

Nutritional Values

- ➤ *Calories 32*
- ➤ *Total Fat 22.1 g*
- ➤ *Saturated Fat 12.7 g*
- ➤ *Cholesterol 53 mg*
- ➤ *Sodium 1,130 mg*
- ➤ *Total Carbs 17.1 g*
- ➤ *Fiber 1.4 g*
- ➤ *Sugar 9.6 g*
- ➤ *Protein 16.1 g*

"LongHorn Steakhouse" Mushroom Truffle Bisque

Ingredients

- ➢ 2 tablespoons butter
- ➢ 4 ounces fresh baby Portobello mushroom, sliced
- ➢ 4 ounces fresh white button mushrooms, sliced

- ➤ ½ cup yellow onion, chopped
- ➤ ½ teaspoon salt
- ➤ 1 teaspoon garlic, chopped
- ➤ 3 cups chicken broth
- ➤ 1 cup heavy cream
- ➤ 1 ½ teaspoons truffle oil

How to Prepare

1. In a medium pan, melt the butter over medium heat and cook the mushrooms and onion with salt for about 5–7 minutes, stirring frequently.
2. Add the garlic, and sauté for about 1–2 minutes.
3. Stir in the broth and remove from the heat.
4. With a stick blender, blend the soup until mushrooms are chopped very finely.
5. In the pan, add the heavy cream and stir to combine.
6. Place the pan over medium heat and cook for about 3–5 minutes.
7. Remove from the heat and stir in the truffle oil.
8. Serve immediately.

Preparation time: 15 minutes
Cooking time: 15 minutes
Total time: 30 minutes
Servings: 4

Nutritional Values

- ➤ *Calories 218*
- ➤ *Total Fat 19.8 g*
- ➤ *Saturated Fat 11.1 g*
- ➤ *Cholesterol 56 mg*
- ➤ *Sodium 919 mg*
- ➤ *Total Carbs 5.5 g*
- ➤ *Fiber 1 g*
- ➤ *Sugar 2.2 g*

➢ *Protein 6.1 g*

"Olive Garden" Zuppa Toscana Soup

Ingredients

- ➤ 16 ounces spicy Italian sausage
- ➤ 8 bacon slices, cut into small pieces
- ➤ ½ large onion, chopped
- ➤ 2–3 garlic cloves, minced
- ➤ 5 medium russet potatoes, sliced thinly

- ➢ 1 teaspoon red pepper flakes, crushed
- ➢ Salt and ground black pepper, to taste
- ➢ 28 ounces low-sodium chicken broth
- ➢ 3 cups water
- ➢ 4 cups fresh kale, tough ribs removed and chopped
- ➢ 1 cup heavy whipping cream
- ➢ ½ cup Parmesan cheese, shredded

How to Prepare

1. Heat a large Dutch oven over medium heat and cook the sausage for about 6–8 minutes, or until browned.
2. With a slotted spoon, transfer the sausage into a bowl and set aside.
3. In the same pan, add the bacon and cook for about 8–10 minutes, or until crispy, stirring occasionally.
4. Stir in the onion and cook for about 5–6 minutes, stirring frequently.
5. Stir in the garlic and cook for about 1 minute, stirring frequently.
6. Stir in the potatoes, red pepper flakes, salt, black pepper, broth, and water, and bring to a boil.
7. Cook for about 10 minutes.
8. Stir in the kale and cook for about 5–10 minutes, stirring occasionally.
9. Stir in the heavy cream and cook for about 2–3 minutes, or until heated through.
10. Serve hot with the garnishing of Parmesan cheese.

Preparation time: 15 minutes
Cooking time: 40 minutes
Total time: 55 minutes
Servings: 8

Nutritional Values

- ➢ *Calories 398*
- ➢ *Total Fat 24.2 g*
- ➢ *Saturated Fat 9.9 g*

- ➢ *Cholesterol 75 mg*
- ➢ *Sodium 647 mg*
- ➢ *Total Carbs 26.7 g*
- ➢ *Fiber 4 g*
- ➢ *Sugar 2 g*
- ➢ *Protein 18.4 g*

"Olive Garden" Chicken Gnocchi Soup

Ingredients

- ➢ 4 tablespoons butter
- ➢ 1 tablespoon extra-virgin olive oil
- ➢ 1 cup onion, chopped finely
- ➢ ½ cup celery, chopped finely
- ➢ 2 garlic cloves, minced

- ➢ ¼ cup all-purpose flour
- ➢ 4 cups half-and-half
- ➢ 28 ounces chicken broth
- ➢ 1 (16-ounce) package ready-to-use gnocchi
- ➢ 1 cup cooked chicken breast, chopped
- ➢ 1 cup fresh spinach leaves, chopped
- ➢ 1 cup carrots, peeled and shredded finely
- ➢ ½ teaspoon dried parsley flakes
- ➢ ½ teaspoon dried thyme
- ➢ ¼ teaspoon ground nutmeg
- ➢ Salt, to taste

How to Prepare

1. In a large soup pan, melt the butter with oil over medium heat and cook the onion, celery, and garlic for about 5–6 minutes, stirring occasionally.
2. Stir in the flour and cook for about 1 minute.
3. Add the half-and-half and beat until well combined.
4. Simmer until thickened, stirring continuously.
5. Stir in the broth and simmer until thickened.
6. Stir in gnocchi, chicken, spinach, carrots, dried herbs, nutmeg and salt and cook for about 3–5 minutes, stirring occasionally.

Preparation time: 15 minutes
Cooking time: 15 minutes
Total time: 30 minutes
Servings: 8

Nutritional Values

- ➢ *Calories 380*
- ➢ *Total Fat 23.1 g*
- ➢ *Saturated Fat 12.9 g*
- ➢ *Cholesterol 74 mg*
- ➢ *Sodium 785 mg*

- ➤ *Total Carbs 29.4 g*
- ➤ *Fiber 2.5 g*
- ➤ *Sugar 1.9 g*
- ➤ *Protein 13.6 g*

"Chili's" Chicken Enchilada Soup

Ingredients

- ➤ 1 tablespoon olive oil
- ➤ 1 medium onion, chopped
- ➤ 2 poblano peppers, chopped finely
- ➤ 3 garlic cloves, minced
- ➤ 1 pound boneless, skinless chicken breasts
- ➤ 1 (14 ½-ounce) can diced tomatoes with juice
- ➤ 1 (10-ounce) can enchilada sauce
- ➤ 2 tablespoons tomato paste

- ➢ ½–1 teaspoon chipotle hot pepper sauce
- ➢ 1 tablespoon chili powder
- ➢ 2 teaspoons ground cumin
- ➢ ½ teaspoon ground black pepper
- ➢ 1 (48-ounce) carton chicken broth
- ➢ 1/3 cup fresh cilantro, minced

How to Prepare

1. In a large skillet, heat the oil over medium heat and cook the onion and poblano peppers for about 8–9 minutes, stirring frequently.
2. Add the garlic and sauté for about 1 minute.
3. In a slow cooker, place the cooked onion mixture and remaining ingredients except for cilantro and stir to combine.
4. Set the slow cooker on low and cook, covered for about 6–8 hours.
5. Uncover the slow cooker and with a slotted spoon, transfer the chicken breasts into a bowl.
6. With 2 forks, shred the meat.
7. Return the shredded meat into the slow cooker with cilantro and stir to combine.
8. Serve hot.

Preparation time: 15 minutes
Cooking time: 8 hours, 10 minutes
Total time: 8 hours, 25 minutes
Servings: 8

Nutritional Values

- ➢ *Calories 270*
- ➢ *Total Fat 8.5 g*
- ➢ *Saturated Fat 2.1 g*
- ➢ *Cholesterol 50 mg*
- ➢ *Sodium 624 mg*
- ➢ *Total Carbs 29.9 g*
- ➢ *Fiber 11.1 g*

> *Sugar 3.8 g*
> *Protein 25 g*

"Carrabba's" Sausage & Lentil Soup

Ingredients

- ➤ 2 tablespoons butter
- ➤ 1 cup white onion, chopped
- ➤ ½ cup celery, chopped
- ➤ ½ cup carrot, chopped
- ➤ 3 garlic cloves, minced

➢ Salt, to taste
➢ 1 pound Italian sausage
➢ 1 cup brown lentils
➢ 48 ounces low-sodium chicken broth
➢ 1 ½ teaspoons Italian seasoning

How to Prepare

1. In a large soup pan, melt butter over medium heat and sauté the onions, celery, carrots, and garlic for about 4–5 minutes.
2. Add the sausage and cook for about 4–5 minutes, or until browned.
3. Drain the excess grease from pan.
4. Add lentils, tomatoes, broth, and Italian seasoning, and bring to a boil over high heat.
5. Reduce the heat to low and simmer, covered for about 1 hour.
6. Stir in salt and serve hot.

Preparation time: 15 minutes
Cooking time: 1 hour, 30 minutes
Total time: 1 hour, 45 minutes
Servings: 8

Nutritional Values

➢ *Calories 327*
➢ *Total Fat 19.5 g*
➢ *Saturated Fat 7.1 g*
➢ *Cholesterol 56 mg*
➢ *Sodium 526 mg*
➢ *Total Carbs 17.8g*
➢ *Fiber 7.9 g*
➢ *Sugar 1.6 g*
➢ *Protein 19 g*

"Pappadeaux" Crawfish Bisque

Ingredients

- 3 pounds crawfish
- ¼ cup olive oil
- 1 teaspoon paprika
- 1/8 teaspoon cayenne pepper
- 4 cups water
- ½ cup green bell pepper, seeded and chopped
- ½ cup onion, chopped

- ➢ ½ cup tomato, chopped
- ➢ 1 tablespoon tomato paste
- ➢ 3 cups whipping cream
- ➢ 4 tablespoons brandy

How to Prepare

1. In a large pan of water, add the crawfish and bring to a rolling boil.
2. Remove from the heat and drain the crawfish. Set aside to cool slightly.
3. Remove the tail meat and transfer into a bowl, reserving the heads and shells in another bowl.
4. In a Dutch oven, heat the oil over medium heat and sauté the crawfish heads, shells, paprika, and cayenne pepper for about 5 minutes.
5. Add the water and bring to a boil.
6. Reduce the heat to low and simmer for about 30 minutes.
7. Remove from the heat and strain the liquid into another large pan.
8. Place the pan over low heat and stir in the bell pepper, onion, tomato, tomato paste, and cream.
9. Simmer for about 1 hour, stirring frequently.
10. Stir in the brandy and the crawfish meat and simmer for 10 minutes.
11. Serve hot.

Preparation time: 15 minutes
Cooking time: 1 hour, 50 minutes
Total time: 2 hours, 5 minutes
Servings: 8

Nutritional Values

- ➢ *Calories 349*
- ➢ *Total Fat 22.5 g*
- ➢ *Saturated Fat 10 g*
- ➢ *Cholesterol 28 mg*

- ➢ *Sodium 187 mg*
- ➢ *Total Carbs 3.7 g*
- ➢ *Fiber 0.6 g*
- ➢ *Sugar 1.4g*
- ➢ *Protein 31.2 g*

CHAPTER 4
CHICKEN & DUCK RECIPES

"Chili's" Santa Fe Chicken Salad

Ingredients

- ¼ teaspoon dried oregano
- 3 teaspoons chili powder
- 1 teaspoon paprika
- 1 teaspoon ground cumin
- 1 teaspoon seasoned salt

- ➢ 1 teaspoon ground black pepper
- ➢ ½ teaspoon ground white pepper
- ➢ ¼ teaspoon red pepper flakes, crushed
- ➢ 1½ pounds boneless, skinless chicken breasts
- ➢ 1 cup chicken broth
- ➢ 9 cups romaine lettuce, torn
- ➢ 1/3 cup cheddar cheese, shredded

How to Prepare

1. In a small bowl, mix together the oregano and spices.
2. Rub the chicken with spice mixture generously.
3. In a slow cooker, place the chicken breasts and pour the broth.
4. Set the slow cooker on low and cook, covered for about 3–4 hours, or until chicken is cooked through.
5. Uncover and transfer the chicken breasts into a bowl. Set aside to cool slightly.
6. With 2 forks, shred the meat.
7. Divide the lettuce onto serving plates and top with shredded chicken.
8. Sprinkle with cheese and serve.

Preparation time: 15 minutes
Cooking time: 4 hours
Total time: 4 hours, 15 minutes
Servings: 6

Nutritional Values

- ➢ *Calories 266*
- ➢ *Total Fat 11.2 g*
- ➢ *Saturated Fat 3.8 g*
- ➢ *Cholesterol 108 mg*
- ➢ *Sodium 536 mg*
- ➢ *Total Carbs 4.1 g*
- ➢ *Fiber 1.3 g*
- ➢ *Sugar 1.1 g*

➤ *Protein 35.9 g*

"Subway" Orchid Chicken Salad

Ingredients

- ➢ 3 cups cooked chicken breast, chopped
- ➢ 1 Granny Smith apple, cored and cubed
- ➢ 1 honey crisp apple, cored and cubed
- ➢ 1 tablespoon fresh lemon juice
- ➢ ½ cup celery, chopped
- ➢ ½ cup cherry juice infused craisins
- ➢ 1 cup light mayonnaise
- ➢ Salt and ground black pepper, to taste

How to Prepare

1. In a bowl, place the apples and drizzle with lemon juice.
2. Add the chicken, celery, and craisins, and mix well.
3. Add the mayonnaise, salt, and black pepper, and gently stir to combine.
4. Cover the bowl and refrigerate for about 1 hour before serving.

Preparation time: 15 minutes
Total time: 15 minutes
Servings: 4

Nutritional Values

- *Calories 503*
- *Total Fat 23.1 g*
- *Saturated Fat 3.8 g*
- *Cholesterol 96 mg*
- *Sodium 536 mg*
- *Total Carbs 44.3 g*
- *Fiber 3.6 g*
- *Sugar 26.3 g*
- *Protein 31.9 g*

"KFC" Crispy Fried Chicken

Ingredients

- ➤ 2 large eggs
- ➤ 1½ cups water
- ➤ 4 cups all-purpose flour, divided
- ➤ 1 teaspoon salt

- ➤ 3 teaspoons ground black pepper, divided
- ➤ 2 tablespoons garlic salt
- ➤ 1 tablespoon paprika
- ➤ 2 ½ teaspoons poultry seasoning
- ➤ 2 (3 ½–4 pounds) fryer chickens cut up
- ➤ 6–8 cups canola oil

How to Prepare

1. In a shallow dish, add eggs, water, 1 1/3 cups of flour, salt and ½ teaspoon of black pepper, and beat until well combined.
2. In another shallow dish, combine remaining flour, garlic salt, paprika, poultry seasoning, and remaining black pepper, and mix well.
3. Dip chicken pieces in egg mixture and then coat with flour mixture.
4. In a deep fryer, heat the oil over medium heat and cook the chicken pieces in 3 batches for about 7–8 minutes per side.
5. With paper towels, transfer the chicken pieces onto a paper towel-lined platter to drain.

Preparation time: 15 minutes
Cooking time: 48 minutes
Total time: 1 hour, 3 minutes
Servings: 14

Nutritional Values

- ➤ *Calories 1,220*
- ➤ *Total Fat 104.2 g*
- ➤ *Saturated Fat 9.8 g*
- ➤ *Cholesterol 142 mg*
- ➤ *Sodium 290 mg*
- ➤ *Total Carbs 28.9 g*
- ➤ *Fiber 1.4 g*
- ➤ *Sugar 0.5 g*
- ➤ *Protein 42.4 g*

"The Cheesecake Factory" Chicken Piccatta

Ingredients

- 1 ½ pounds chicken breasts
- Salt, to taste
- ½ teaspoon ground black pepper
- 1 tablespoon oil
- 5 tablespoons plus 2 teaspoons butter, divided

- ➢ 8 ounces fresh Portobello mushrooms, sliced
- ➢ ¼ cup dry white wine
- ➢ 1 tablespoon fresh lemon juice
- ➢ 2 tablespoons heavy cream
- ➢ 1 tablespoon capers
- ➢ 2 teaspoons fresh parsley, chopped

How to Prepare

1. Cut each chicken breast in half and pound into ¼-inch thickness.
2. Season each chicken breast with salt and black pepper evenly.
3. In a wok, heat oil and 1 tablespoon butter over medium heat and cook chicken breasts for about 4–5 minutes per side, or until browned.
4. With a slotted spoon, transfer the chicken breasts onto a plate.
5. In the same wok, add 1 tablespoon of butter, mushrooms and a pinch salt and sauté for about 4–5 minutes.
6. With a slotted spoon, transfer the mushrooms onto a plate.
7. In the wok, add wine and with a wooden spoon, scrape the browned bits from the bottom.
8. Add the remaining butter and lemon juice and stir to combine.
9. Add the heavy cream and capers and stir to combine.
10. Increase the heat to medium-high and cook until the mixture begins to bubble.
11. Stir in the chicken, mushrooms and parsley and remove from the heat.
12. Serve immediately.

Preparation time: 15 minutes
Cooking time: 20 minutes
Total time: 35 minutes
Servings: 4

Nutritional Values

- ➤ *Calories 533*
- ➤ *Total Fat 33.4 g*
- ➤ *Saturated Fat 14.8 g*
- ➤ *Cholesterol 200 mg*
- ➤ *Sodium 359 mg*
- ➤ *Total Carbs 2.9 g*
- ➤ *Fiber 0.8 g*
- ➤ *Sugar 1.2 g*
- ➤ *Protein 51.4 g*

"Outback Steakhouse" Alice Spring Chicken

Ingredients

<u>Sauce</u>

- ½ cup honey
- ½ cup Dijon mustard
- ¼ cup mayonnaise
- 1 teaspoon fresh lemon juice

<u>**Chicken**</u>

- ➤ 4 (6-ounce) boneless, skinless chicken breasts
- ➤ 2 tablespoons butter
- ➤ 8 ounces fresh mushrooms, sliced
- ➤ 1 tablespoon olive oil
- ➤ 4 cooked bacon slices, cut into 2-inch pieces
- ➤ 2 cups Colby Jack cheese, shredded
- ➤ 2 tablespoons fresh parsley, chopped

How to Prepare

1. **Sauce:** In a small bowl, add all ingredients and beat until well combined.
2. Place ¼ cup of sauce in a covered container and refrigerate until using.
3. In a large Ziploc bag, place the chicken breast and remaining sauce.
4. Seal the bag and shake to coat well.
5. Refrigerate for 30–60 minutes.
6. Preheat oven to 400°F.
7. In a large oven-proof skillet, melt butter over medium-high heat and sauté the mushrooms for about 5–7 minutes.
8. With a slotted spoon, transfer the mushrooms into a bowl.
9. With paper towels, wipe out the skillet.
10. Remove the chicken breasts from bag and discard the marinade.
11. In the same skillet, heat the oil over medium heat.
12. Place the chicken breasts in a single layer and cook for about 5 minutes, without moving.
13. Flip the chicken breasts and cook for about 5 minutes.
14. Arrange the mushrooms over chicken breasts evenly, followed by the bacon and cheese.
15. Cover the skillet and immediately transfer into the oven.
16. Bake for about 10–15 minutes.
17. Remove from the oven and set aside for about 5 minutes.

18. Serve with the garnishing of parsley alongside the reserved sauce on the side for dipping.

Preparation time: 15 minutes
Cooking time: 32 minutes
Total time: 47 minutes
Servings: 4

Nutritional Values

➢ *Calories 872*
➢ *Total Fat 50 g*
➢ *Saturated Fat 20.9 g*
➢ *Cholesterol 210 mg*
➢ *Sodium 1,600 mg*
➢ *Total Carbs 44.5 g*
➢ *Fiber 1.8 g*
➢ *Sugar 37 g*
➢ *Protein 62.3 g*

"The Cheesecake Factory" Orange Chicken

Ingredients

Chicken

- 2 eggs
- 1 ½ cups all-purpose flour
- Salt and ground black pepper, to taste
- 2 pounds boneless, skinless chicken breasts, cut into 1 ½-inch cubes

➤ 1–2 cups canola oil

<u>Orange Sauce</u>
➤ 1 ¾ cups water, divided
➤ ¼ cup fresh lemon juice
➤ 2 tablespoons fresh orange juice
➤ 2 ½ tablespoons soy sauce
➤ 1 tablespoon orange peel, grated
➤ 1 cup packed brown sugar
➤ ½ teaspoon ginger, minced
➤ ½ teaspoon garlic powder
➤ ¼ teaspoon red pepper flakes
➤ 3 tablespoons cornstarch

How to Prepare

1. In a shallow bowl, beat the eggs.
2. In a separate bowl, place flour, salt, and black pepper, and mix well.
3. Dip the chicken cubes in eggs and then coat with flour mixture.
4. In a deep skillet, heat the oil over medium-high heat and fry the chicken cubes in 3 batches for about 3–5 minutes, or until cooked through.
5. With a slotted spoon, transfer the chicken cubes onto a paper towel-lined plate to drain.
6. In a large saucepan, add 1 ½ cups water, lemon juice, orange juice and soy sauce over medium heat and cook for about 2–4 minutes.
7. Stir in the brown sugar, orange zest, ginger, and garlic powder, and bring to a boil.
8. Meanwhile, in a small bowl, dissolve the cornstarch in water.
9. In the wok, add the cornstarch mixture, stirring continuously until smooth.
10. Stir in the chicken and red pepper flakes and remove from the heat.
11. Serve hot.

Preparation time: 15 minutes

Cooking time: 25 minutes
Total time: 40 minutes
Servings: 6

Nutritional Values

- *Calories 861*
- *Total Fat 49.4 g*
- *Saturated Fat 6.3 g*
- *Cholesterol 189 mg*
- *Sodium 566 mg*
- *Total Carbs 5.2 g*
- *Fiber 1.2 g*
- *Sugar 24.5 g*
- *Protein 49.5 g*

"Carrabba's" Chicken Bryan

Ingredients

- ➢ 4 (6-ounce) chicken breasts
- ➢ ½ teaspoon salt
- ➢ ¼ teaspoon ground black pepper
- ➢ 2 tablespoons olive oil
- ➢ 8 ounces goat cheese, cut into 4 slices
- ➢ 8 tablespoons butter, divided
- ➢ ¾ cup dry white wine

- ➢ 2 tablespoons fresh lemon juice
- ➢ ¼ cup onion, chopped
- ➢ 2 teaspoons garlic, chopped
- ➢ 2 tablespoons fresh basil, sliced thinly
- ➢ 2 tablespoons sun-dried tomatoes

How to Prepare

1. Preheat the grill to medium-high heat.
2. Grease the grill grate.
3. With a meat mallet, pound the chicken breasts thinly.
4. Season each chicken with salt and black pepper and then brush with oil.
5. Place the chicken breasts onto the grill and cook for about 3–4 minutes per side.
6. Remove from the grill and place the chicken breasts onto a plate.
7. With plastic wrap, cover the chicken breasts lightly to keep warm.
8. **Sauce:** In a skillet, melt 2 tablespoons of butter over medium heat and sauté the onions and garlic for about 4–5 minutes.
9. Stir in the wine and lemon juice and simmer for about 2–3 minutes.
10. Add 3 tablespoons of butter and beat until melted completely.
11. Remove from the heat and add the remaining butter, beating continuously until melted completely.
12. Through a strainer, strain the butter sauce.
13. Return the sauce into the skillet and stir in half of the basil and sun-dried tomatoes.
14. Divide the chicken breast onto serving plates and top each with a goat cheese slice.
15. Pour the sauce over each chicken breast and serve with the garnishing of remaining basil.

Preparation time: 15 minutes
Cooking time: 20 minutes
Total time: 35 minutes

Servings: 4

Nutritional Values

- *Calories 782*
- *Total Fat 54.8 g*
- *Saturated Fat 27.6 g*
- *Cholesterol 263 mg*
- *Sodium 1,200 mg*
- *Total Carbs 5.2 g*
- *Fiber 0.3 g*
- *Sugar 3.3 g*
- *Protein 57.9 g*

"P.F. Chang's" Kung Pao Chicken

Ingredients

<u>Sauce</u>
- ➢ ½ cup chicken broth
- ➢ ¼ cup low-sodium soy sauce
- ➢ 1 teaspoon sesame oil
- ➢ 1 teaspoon balsamic vinegar
- ➢ 1 teaspoon chili garlic sauce

- ➢ 1 tablespoon brown sugar
- ➢ 2 garlic cloves, minced
- ➢ ½ teaspoon ginger paste

Chicken

- ➢ 1 ½ pounds boneless chicken thighs, cut into 1-inch pieces
- ➢ Salt and ground black pepper, to taste
- ➢ 2 tablespoons coconut oil
- ➢ 1 bell pepper, seeded and sliced
- ➢ 3 dried red chiles
- ➢ ¼ cup peanuts

How to Prepare

1. **Sauce:** In a small bowl, add all the ingredients and beat until well combined. Set aside.
2. Season the chicken thighs with a little salt and black pepper.
3. In a skillet, melt the coconut oil over medium-high heat and cook the chicken thighs for about 3 minutes per side.
4. Stir in the bell pepper and dried chiles and cook for about 4–5 minutes.
5. Add the peanuts and sauce and stir to combine.
6. Increase the heat to high and cook for about 2–3 minutes, stirring continuously.
7. Serve hot.

Preparation time: 15 minutes
Cooking time: 15 minutes
Total time: 30 minutes
Servings: 4

Nutritional Values

- ➢ *Calories 513*
- ➢ *Total Fat 38.3 g*
- ➢ *Saturated Fat 14.2 g*

➢ Cholesterol 143 mg
➢ Sodium 1,100 mg
➢ Total Carbs 7.7 g
➢ Fiber 1.2 g
➢ Sugar 5.2 g
➢ Protein 4.5 g

"Olive Garden" Chicken Parmigiana

Ingredients

- ➢ 12 ounces frozen grilled chicken breast strips
- ➢ 1 (14 ½-ounces) can diced tomatoes with juice
- ➢ 1 (6 ounces) can tomato paste
- ➢ 2 tablespoons dry red wine
- ➢ 1 tablespoon olive oil
- ➢ 1 ½ teaspoons Italian seasoning

- ➤ 1 garlic clove, minced
- ➤ ½ teaspoon sugar
- ➤ 1/3 cup Parmesan cheese, shredded
- ➤ 1/3 cup part-skim mozzarella cheese, shredded

How to Prepare

1. Heat a lightly greased large wok over medium heat and cook the chicken strips for about 5–8 minutes, or until heated through.
2. With a slotted spoon, transfer the chicken strips onto a plate.
3. In the same wok, add the remaining ingredients except for cheese and bring to a boil, stirring occasionally.
4. Reduce the heat to low and simmer, uncovered for about 10–15 minutes, stirring occasionally.
5. Stir in chicken strips and sprinkle with both cheeses.
6. Cover the wok and cook for about 1–2 minutes, or until cheese is melted.
7. Serve hot.

Preparation time: 15 minutes
Cooking time: 30 minutes
Total time: 45 minutes
Servings: 4

Nutritional Values

- ➤ *Calories 229*
- ➤ *Total Fat 8.8 g*
- ➤ *Saturated Fat 2.1 g*
- ➤ *Cholesterol 62 mg*
- ➤ *Sodium 218 mg*
- ➤ *Total Carbs 13.5 g*
- ➤ *Fiber 3 g*
- ➤ *Sugar 8.6 g*
- ➤ *Protein 24 g*

"California Pizza Kitchen" Chicken Pizza

Ingredients

- ➢ 1 pound refrigerated pizza dough, divided into 2 pieces
- ➢ 2 cups cooked chicken, shredded
- ➢ ¾ cup barbecue sauce, divided
- ➢ 1 cup mozzarella cheese, shredded
- ➢ ¼ of medium red onion, sliced thinly
- ➢ 1/3 cup Gouda cheese, shredded

- ➢ Pinch of red pepper flakes, crushed
- ➢ 2 tablespoons fresh cilantro, chopped

How to Prepare

1. Preheat the oven to 500°F.
2. Line 2 large baking sheets with greased parchment paper.
3. In a medium bowl, add chicken and ¼ cup of barbecue sauce and mix well.
4. Place each pizza dough onto a lightly floured surface and roll into a large circle.
5. Place 1 dough circle onto 1 of each prepared baking sheet.
6. Spread barbecue sauce over each dough and top with chicken mixture, leaving 1-inch around the edges.
7. Place a layer of mozzarella on top, followed by red onion, Gouda cheese.
8. Sprinkle with red pepper flakes evenly.
9. Bake for about 20–25 minutes.
10. Garnish with cilantro and serve.

Preparation time: 15 minutes
Cooking time: 25 minutes
Total time: 40 minutes
Servings: 8

Nutritional Values

- ➢ *Calories 372*
- ➢ *Total Fat 19.7 g*
- ➢ *Saturated Fat 5.4 g*
- ➢ *Cholesterol 29 mg*
- ➢ *Sodium 595 mg*
- ➢ *Total Carbs 33 g*
- ➢ *Fiber 2.2 g*
- ➢ *Sugar 6.4 g*
- ➢ *Protein 14.8 g*

CHAPTER 5

BEEF & PORK RECIPES

"McDonald's" Big Mac Salad

Ingredients

Dressing

- ➢ ¾ cup mayonnaise
- ➢ 2 tablespoons dill pickles

- ➤ 1 tablespoon onions, chopped
- ➤ 4 teaspoons prepared mustard
- ➤ 1 tablespoon white vinegar
- ➤ 2 teaspoons sugar
- ➤ ½ teaspoon smoked paprika

Salad

- ➤ 1 pound lean ground beef
- ➤ Kosher salt and ground black pepper, to taste
- ➤ 4 cups iceberg lettuce, chopped
- ➤ ½ cup onions, sliced
- ➤ ¼ cup dill pickles, chopped roughly
- ➤ 1 cup sharp cheddar cheese, shredded

How to Prepare

1. **Dressing:** In a bowl, add all ingredients and mix until well combined. Set aside.
2. Heat a 10-inch sauté pan over medium heat and cook the ground beef for about 8–10 minutes, breaking up the meat with a wooden spoon.
3. Stir in the salt and black pepper and cook for about 1–2 minutes.
4. Remove from the heat and set aside to cool slightly.
5. Divide beef, lettuce, onion, dill pickles, and cheese into serving bowls evenly.
6. Drizzle with dressing and serve.

Preparation time: 15 minutes
Cooking time: 12 minutes
Total time: 27 minutes
Servings: 4

Nutritional Values

- ➤ *Calories 519*
- ➤ *Total Fat 31.5 g*
- ➤ *Saturated Fat 10.8 g*

- ➢ *Cholesterol 142 mg*
- ➢ *Sodium 838 mg*
- ➢ *Total Carbs 15.5 g*
- ➢ *Fiber 0.9 g*
- ➢ *Sugar 5.9 g*
- ➢ *Protein 42.4 g*

"Wendy's" Chili

Ingredients

- ➢ 2 tablespoons olive oil
- ➢ 3 pounds ground beef
- ➢ 1 cup yellow onion, chopped finely
- ➢ ½ cup celery, chopped finely
- ➢ ½ cup green bell pepper, seeded and chopped finely
- ➢ ½ cup red bell pepper, seeded and chopped finely
- ➢ 1 (15-ounce) can crushed tomatoes with juice
- ➢ 1 ½ cups tomato juice
- ➢ 1 ½ teaspoons Worcestershire sauce
- ➢ ½ teaspoon dried oregano

- ➤ 2 teaspoons sugar
- ➤ 3 tablespoons red chili powder
- ➤ 1 teaspoon ground cumin
- ➤ 1 teaspoon garlic powder
- ➤ 1 teaspoon salt
- ➤ ½ teaspoon ground black pepper

How to Prepare

1. In a large pan, heat the oil over medium-high heat and cook the beef for about 8–10 minutes or until browned.
2. Drain the grease from pan, leaving about 2 tablespoons inside.
3. In the pan, add the onions, celery and bell peppers over medium-high heat and cook for about 5 minutes, stirring frequently.
4. Add the tomatoes, tomato juice, Worcestershire sauce, oregano, sugar, and spices, and stir to combine.
5. Reduce the heat to low and simmer, covered for about 1–1 ½ hours, stirring occasionally.
6. Serve hot.

Preparation time: 15 minutes
Cooking time: 1 hour, 45 minutes
Total time: 2 hours
Servings: 8

Nutritional Values

- ➤ *Calories 403*
- ➤ *Total Fat 14.7 g*
- ➤ *Saturated Fat 4.6 g*
- ➤ *Cholesterol 152 mg*
- ➤ *Sodium 673 mg*
- ➤ *Total Carbs 12.1 g*
- ➤ *Fiber 3.6 g*
- ➤ *Sugar 7.5 g*
- ➤ *Protein 54.1 g*

"P.F. Chang's China Bistro" Mongolian Beef

Ingredients

Sauce

- ½ cup brown sugar
- ½ cup water
- ¼ cup low-sodium soy sauce
- 2 teaspoons canola oil

➢ 3 garlic cloves, minced
➢ 2 teaspoons fresh ginger, grated

Beef

➢ 1 pound flank steak, cut into thin slices across the grain
➢ ¼ cup cornstarch
➢ ½ cup canola oil
➢ 2 scallions, sliced thinly

How to Prepare

1. **Sauce:** In a medium bowl, add all ingredients and beat until well combined.
2. In a medium saucepan, add sauce over medium-low heat and cook for about 5–10 minutes or until slightly thickened, stirring frequently.
3. Remove the saucepan of sauce from heat and set aside.
4. In a large bowl, add flank steak and cornstarch and toss to coat well.
5. Heat the vegetable oil in a large saucepan over medium-high heat and sear the steak slices for about 2 minutes.
6. With a slotted spoon, transfer the steak slices onto a paper towel-lined plate to drain.
7. Add the steak slices into the pan of sauce and stir to combine.
8. Place the saucepan over medium heat and cook for about 2–3 minutes, or until sauce thickens.
9. Stir in scallions and serve immediately.

Preparation time: 15 minutes
Cooking time: 15 minutes
Total time: 30 minutes
Servings: 4

Nutritional Values

➢ *Calories 594*
➢ *Total Fat 39.8 g*
➢ *Saturated Fat 6.1 g*

- ➢ *Cholesterol 62 mg*
- ➢ *Sodium 952 mg*
- ➢ *Total Carbs 28 g*
- ➢ *Fiber 0.4 g*
- ➢ *Sugar 18.8 g*
- ➢ *Protein 33 g*

"The Cheesecake Factory" Steak Diane

Ingredients

- ➢ 12 ounces beef tenderloin, cut into 3-ounce medallions
- ➢ Salt, to taste
- ➢ 2 teaspoons cracked black peppercorns
- ➢ 2 tablespoons butter
- ➢ ½ cup fresh mushrooms, sliced

- ➢ 3 tablespoons pearl onions, chopped
- ➢ ¼ cup white wine
- ➢ 1 tablespoon Dijon mustard
- ➢ 1 teaspoon Worcestershire sauce
- ➢ ¾ cup beef broth
- ➢ ¼ cup cream

How to Prepare

1. Season the beef with salt and black pepper evenly.
2. In a large heavy skillet, melt 1 tablespoon of butter over medium heat and sear the beef medallions for about 2–3 minutes per side, or until desired doneness.
3. With a slotted spoon, transfer the beef medallions onto a plate and cover them with a piece of foil to keep warm.
4. In the same skillet, melt the remaining butter and cook the pearl onions for about 2 minutes.
5. Add the mushrooms and sauté for about 1–2 minutes.
6. Add the wine and Worcestershire sauce and bring to a boil.
7. Stir in the mustard and cook for about 1 minute.
8. Stir in the broth and cook for about 1 minute.
9. Stir in the cream and bring to a boil.
10. Immediately, remove from the heat and stir in the chives.
11. Place the mushroom sauce over the beef medallions and serve.

Preparation time: 15 minutes
Cooking time: 15 minutes
Total time: 30 minutes
Servings: 2

Nutritional Values

- ➢ *Calories 528*
- ➢ *Total Fat 29.6 g*
- ➢ *Saturated Fat 14.4 g*

- ➢ *Cholesterol 193 mg*
- ➢ *Sodium 675 mg*
- ➢ *Total Carbs 5 g*
- ➢ *Fiber 0.8 g*
- ➢ *Sugar 2.6 g*
- ➢ *Protein 52.5 g*

"Boston Market" Meatloaf

Ingredients

- ➤ 1 pound lean ground beef
- ➤ 1 egg
- ➤ 1/3 cup ketchup, divided
- ➤ 2 tablespoons sour cream
- ➤ 2 tablespoons flour
- ➤ 1 (1 ½-ounce) envelope dry onion soup mix
- ➤ 1/3 cup spicy hot V8 vegetable juice

How to Prepare

1. Preheat the oven to 400°F.
2. Lightly, grease a loaf pan.
3. In a bowl, add ground beef, egg, 2 tablespoons of ketchup, sour cream, flour, and onion soup mix, and mix until well combined.
4. Place the mixture into the prepared loaf pan.
5. Bake for about 15 minutes.
6. Remove the loaf pan from oven and discard excess grease from loaf.
7. Spread remaining ketchup on top of the loaf and pour V-8 juice around the edges.
8. Bake for about 30 minutes more.
9. Remove the loaf pan from oven and set aside for about 5 minutes before serving.

Preparation time: 15 minutes
Cooking time: 45 minutes
Total time: 1 hour
Servings: 3

Nutritional Values

➢ *Calories 410*
➢ *Total Fat 12.8 g*
➢ *Saturated Fat 5.1 g*
➢ *Cholesterol 193 mg*
➢ *Sodium 1,600 mg*
➢ *Total Carbs 21.6 g*
➢ *Fiber 1.4 g*
➢ *Sugar 7.8 g*
➢ *Protein 50.2 g*

"Café Rio" Sweet Pork

Ingredients

- ➤ 2 pounds boneless pork ribs
- ➤ 3 (12-ounce) cans Coke
- ➤ 1 ¼ cups brown sugar, divided
- ➤ Pinch of garlic salt
- ➤ ¼ cup water
- ➤ 10 ounces red enchilada sauce
- ➤ 1 (6-ounce) can diced green chilies

How to Prepare

1. In a heavy duty Ziploc bag, add pork, 1 ½ cans of Coke and ¼ cup of brown sugar.
2. Seal the bag and shake to coat well.
3. Refrigerate to marinate overnight.
4. Remove the pork from bag and discard the marinade.
5. In a crockpot, place pork ½ can of Coke, water, and garlic salt.
6. Set the crockpot on high and cook, covered for about 3–4 hours.
7. With a slotted spoon, transfer the pork ribs into a bowl and discard the liquid from pot.
8. With 2 forks, shred the meat.
9. In a food processor, ass ½ can of coke, enchilada sauce chilies and remaining brown sugar and pulse until well combined and smooth.
10. In crockpot, place shredded pork and sauce and mix well.
11. Set the crockpot on low and cook, covered for about 2 hours.
12. Serve hot.

Preparation time: 15 minutes
Cooking time: 6 hours
Total time: 6 hours, 15 minutes
Servings: 6

Nutritional Values

➤ *Calories 607*
➤ *Total Fat 8.5 g*
➤ *Saturated Fat 2.5 g*
➤ *Cholesterol 110 mg*
➤ *Sodium 148 mg*
➤ *Total Carbs 96.4 g*
➤ *Fiber 20.7 g*
➤ *Sugar 56.5 g*
➤ *Protein 47.9 g*

"Olive Garden" Pork Filettino

Ingredients

- ➢ 4 garlic cloves
- ➢ 2 tablespoons fresh rosemary, chopped
- ➢ 1 tablespoon fresh sage, chopped
- ➢ 6 tablespoons extra-virgin olive oil
- ➢ Salt and ground black pepper, to taste
- ➢ 4 small pork tenderloins
- ➢ 4 medium russet potatoes, cut into 1-inch pieces

How to Prepare

1. Preheat the oven to 375°F.
2. In a large bowl, add the garlic, fresh herbs, oil, salt, and black pepper, and mix well.
3. Add the pork tenderloins and coat with herb mixture evenly.
4. Set aside for about 30 minutes.
5. Preheat the grill to medium-high heat.
6. Grease the grill grate.
7. Arrange the potatoes onto a baking sheet and roast for about 30 minutes.
8. Place the pork tenderloins onto the grill and cook for about 4–5 minutes per side.
9. Remove from the grill and place the pork tenderloins onto a cutting board.
10. Cut each pork tenderloin into desired-sized slices and serve alongside the potatoes.

Preparation time: 15 minutes
Cooking time: 30 minutes
Total time: 45 minutes
Servings: 4

Nutritional Values

➤ *Calories 680*
➤ *Total Fat 35.3 g*
➤ *Saturated Fat 8.2 g*
➤ *Cholesterol 160 mg*
➤ *Sodium 162 mg*
➤ *Total Carbs 35.8 g*
➤ *Fiber 6.1 g*
➤ *Sugar 2.5 g*
➤ *Protein 54.7 g*

"Outback Steakhouse" Grilled Pork Chops

Ingredients

- ➢ 7 tablespoons olive oil, divided
- ➢ 4 (1-pound) 2-inch thick pork chops
- ➢ ½ cup balsamic vinegar
- ➢ 3 garlic cloves, mashed
- ➢ 1 large sprig fresh rosemary

- ➢ 1 small bunch fresh parsley
- ➢ 1 small bunch fresh thyme
- ➢ 1 tablespoon mustard
- ➢ 1 tablespoon sugar
- ➢ 2 tablespoons kosher salt
- ➢ 1 teaspoon ground black pepper

How to Prepare

1. In a large Ziploc bag, add 4 tablespoons of oil and remaining ingredients and seal the bag.
2. Shake the bag vigorously to coat well and refrigerate overnight.
3. Preheat the one side of grill to high heat and the other to low.
4. Grease the grill grate.
5. Remove the chops from bag and discard the marinade.
6. With paper towels, pat dry the chops and then brush with the remaining oil.
7. Place the chops on hot side of the grill and cook for about 2–3 minutes.
8. Flip the chops and cook for about 2 minutes.
9. Again flip the chops and cook for about 2 more minutes.
10. Now, place the chops on cool side of the grill and cook, covered for about 22–25 minutes or until desired doneness.
11. Remove from the grill and place the chops onto a patter for about 10 minutes before serving.

Preparation time: 10 minutes
Cooking time: 32 minutes
Total time: 42 minutes
Servings: 4

Nutritional Values
- ➢ *Calories 857*
- ➢ *Total Fat 56.8 g*

- *Saturated Fat 17.7 g*
- *Cholesterol 290 mg*
- *Sodium 900 mg*
- *Total Carbs 5.9 g*
- *Fiber 0.4g*
- *Sugar 3.1 g*
- *Protein 85.5 g*

"Olive Garden" Roast Pork with Grapes & Wine

Ingredients

- ➢ 4 tablespoons extra-virgin olive oil, divided
- ➢ 3 tablespoons fresh sage, chopped
- ➢ 3 teaspoons garlic, chopped
- ➢ Salt and ground black pepper, to taste
- ➢ 3 pounds boneless pork loin
- ➢ 1 cup dry white wine
- ➢ 1 pound red seedless grapes

How to Prepare

1. Preheat the oven to 375°F.
2. Grease a baking dish.
3. In a bowl, add 2 tablespoons of oil, garlic, sage, salt, and black pepper, and mix well.
4. Add the pork loin and coat with the mixture generously.
5. Place the pork loin into the prepared baking dish.
6. With a piece of foil, cover the baking dish and roast for about 45 minutes.
7. Remove from the oven and place the pork tenderloin onto a cutting board for 10 minutes before slicing.
8. Place the pan drippings in a pan over medium heat.
9. Add the wine and grapes and cook for about 3–5 minutes.
10. Cut the pork into desired sized slices and serve with the topping of grapes mixture.

Preparation time: 15 minutes
Cooking time: 50 minutes
Total time: 1 hour, 5 minutes
Servings: 8

Nutritional Values

➢ *Calories 539*
➢ *Total Fat 30.8 g*
➢ *Saturated Fat 10 g*
➢ *Cholesterol 136 mg*
➢ *Sodium 128 mg*
➢ *Total Carbs 11.8 g*
➢ *Fiber 0.7 g*
➢ *Sugar 8.9 g*
➢ *Protein 47 g*

"Chipotle Mexican Grill" Pork Carnitas

Ingredients

- 5 pounds pork shoulder
- 2 tablespoons olive oil
- 2 teaspoon kosher salt, divided
- 2 teaspoon ground black pepper, divided
- 4 dried bay leaves

- ➢ ½ cup water
- ➢ 1 tablespoon dried rosemary
- ➢ ½ teaspoon dried thyme, crushed

How to Prepare

1. Rinse the pork shoulder under cold running water thoroughly.
2. With paper towels, pat dry the pork shoulder completely.
3. Season the pork shoulder with 1 teaspoon of salt and 1 teaspoon of black pepper evenly.
4. In a Dutch oven, heat 2 tablespoons of olive oil over medium-high heat and sear the pork shoulder for about 3–4 minutes per side or until browned from all sides.
5. With a slotted spoon, remove the pork shoulder from pan and set aside.
6. In the pan, add water over medium-high heat and bring to a bowl, scraping the browned bits from the bottom with a wooden spoon.
7. In the bottom of slow cooker, place by leaves and top with place pork, followed by the pan liquid from Dutch oven.
8. Sprinkle the top with herbs and remaining salt and black pepper and stir well.
9. Set the slow cooker on low and cook, covered for about 10–12 hours.
10. Remove the lid and with 2 forks, shred the meat.
11. With the spoon, mix the shredded meat with pan sauce.
12. Set the slow cooker on high and cook, covered for about 30–60 minutes.
13. Serve hot.

Preparation time: 15 minutes
Cooking time: 13 hours 8 minutes
Total time: 13 hours 33 minutes
Servings: 12

Nutritional Values

- ➢ *Calories 574*
- ➢ *Total Fat 42.8 g*
- ➢ *Saturated Fat 15.2 g*
- ➢ *Cholesterol 170 mg*
- ➢ *Sodium 517 mg*
- ➢ *Total Carbs 0.4 g*
- ➢ *Fiber 0.2 g*
- ➢ *Sugar 0 g*
- ➢ *Protein 44.1 g*

CHAPTER 6
FISH & SEAFOOD RECIPES

"Red Lobster" Soy Ginger Salmon

Ingredients

- ➢ 1/3 cup low-sodium soy sauce
- ➢ 1/3 cup orange juice
- ➢ ¼ cup honey
- ➢ 1 scallion, chopped
- ➢ 1 teaspoon garlic powder

- ➤ 1 teaspoon ground ginger
- ➤ 1 (1½ pound) ¾-inch thick salmon fillet

How to Prepare

1. **Marinade:** In a bowl, add all ingredients (except for salmon) and mix well.
2. In a shallow bowl, add salmon and 2/3 cup of marinade and mix well.
3. Refrigerate to marinate for about 30 minutes, flipping occasionally.
4. Reserve the remaining marinade.
5. Preheat the barbecue grill to medium heat.
6. Grease the grill grate.
7. Place the salmon fillets onto grill, skin-side down and cook, covered for about 15–18 minutes per side.
8. During the last 5 minutes of cooking, baste the salmon fillet with reserved marinade.
9. Remove the salmon fillets from grill and place onto a cutting board.
10. Cut the salmon into desired-sized fillets and serve.

Preparation time: 15 minutes
Cooking time: 18 minutes
Total time: 33 minutes
Servings: 4

Nutritional Values

- ➤ *Calories 311*
- ➤ *Total Fat 10.6 g*
- ➤ *Saturated Fat 1.5 g*
- ➤ *Cholesterol 75 mg*
- ➤ *Sodium 1,020 mg*
- ➤ *Total Carbs 22.1 g*
- ➤ *Fiber 0.3 g*
- ➤ *Sugar 20.7 g*
- ➤ *Protein 34.8 g*

"Applebee's" Honey Grilled Salmon

Ingredients
- 4 teaspoons olive oil, divided
- ¼ cup dark brown sugar, packed
- ¼ cup pineapple juice
- 2 tablespoons fresh lemon juice
- 2 tablespoons white distilled vinegar
- ½ teaspoon paprika
- ½ teaspoon cayenne pepper

➤ ¼ teaspoon garlic powder
➤ Salt and ground black pepper, to taste
➤ 4 salmon fillets

How to Prepare

1. In a saucepan, add 2 teaspoons of oil and remaining ingredients (except for salmon fillets) over medium-low heat and bring to a boil, stirring occasionally.
2. Reduce the heat to low and simmer, uncovered for about 15 minutes, stirring occasionally.
3. Preheat the barbecue grill to medium heat.
4. Grease the grill grate.
5. Rub the salmon fillets with remaining olive oil and then sprinkle with salt and black pepper lightly.
6. Place the salmon fillets onto grill and cook for about 3–4 minutes per side.
7. Remove the salmon fillets from grill and brush each fillet with the honey sauce.
8. Serve hot.

Preparation time: 15 minutes
Cooking time: 23 minutes
Total time: 38 minutes
Servings: 4

Nutritional Values

➤ *Calories 274*
➤ *Total Fat 13.6 g*
➤ *Saturated Fat 2 g*
➤ *Cholesterol 63 mg*
➤ *Sodium 202 mg*
➤ *Total Carbs 11.5 g*
➤ *Fiber 0.2 g*
➤ *Sugar 10.6 g*

➢ *Protein 27.7 g*

"Olive Garden" Tilapia Piccata

Ingredients

- ➢ 3 tablespoons fresh lemon juice
- ➢ 2 tablespoons olive oil
- ➢ 2 garlic cloves, minced
- ➢ ½ teaspoon lemon zest, grated
- ➢ 2 teaspoons capers, drained
- ➢ 3 tablespoons fresh basil, minced and divided
- ➢ 4 (6-ounce) tilapia fillets
- ➢ Salt and ground black pepper, to taste

How to Prepare

1. Preheat the broiler of the oven.
2. Arrange an oven rack about 4-inch from the heating element.
3. Grease a broiler pan.
4. In a small bowl, add the lemon juice, oil, garlic, and lemon zest, and beat until well combined.
5. Add the capers and 2 tablespoons of basil and stir to combine.
6. Reserve 2 tablespoons of mixture in a small bowl.
7. Coat the fish fillets with remaining capers mixture and sprinkle with salt and black pepper.
8. Place the tilapia fillets onto the broiler pan and broil for about 3–4 minutes per side.
9. Remove from the oven and place the fish fillets onto serving plates.
10. Drizzle with reserved capers mixture and serve with the garnishing of remaining basil.

Preparation time: 15 minutes
Cooking time: 8 minutes
Total time: 23 minutes
Servings: 4

Nutritional Values

- *Calories 206*
- *Total Fat 8.7 g*
- *Saturated Fat 1.8 g*
- *Cholesterol 83mg*
- *Sodium 144 mg*
- *Total Carbs 0.9 g*
- *Fiber 0.2g*
- *Sugar 0.3 g*
- *Protein 31.9 g*

"Bonefish Grill" Pan-Fried Tilapia with Chimichurri Sauce

![image]

Ingredients

Tilapia
- 4 tilapia fillets
- 2 tablespoons BBQ seasoning

➢ Salt and ground black pepper, to taste
➢ 2 teaspoons olive oil

Chimichurri Sauce

➢ 8 garlic cloves, minced
➢ Salt, to taste
➢ 1 teaspoon dried oregano
➢ 1 teaspoon ground black pepper
➢ 1 teaspoon red pepper flakes, crushed
➢ 4–5 teaspoons lemon zest, grated finely
➢ 4 ounces fresh lemon juice
➢ 1 bunch fresh flat leaf parsley
➢ 1 cup olive oil

How to Prepare

1. **Chimichurri sauce:** In a food processor, add all ingredients and pulse until well combined.
2. Transfer the sauce into a bowl and refrigerate to marinate for 30 minutes before serving.
3. **Tilapia:** Season each tilapia fillet with BBQ seasoning, salt, and black pepper.
4. In a non-stick pan, heat oil over medium-high heat and cook the tilapia fillets for about 3–4 minutes per side, or until cooked through.
5. Divide tilapia fillets onto serving plates.
6. Top each fillet with Chimichurri sauce and serve.

Preparation time: 20 minutes
Cooking time: 8 minutes
Total time: 28 minutes
Servings: 4

Nutritional Values

➢ *Calories 590*
➢ *Total Fat 54.4 g*

- ➤ *Saturated Fat 8.4 g*
- ➤ *Cholesterol 69 mg*
- ➤ *Sodium 786 mg*
- ➤ *Total Carbs 3.8 g*
- ➤ *Fiber 0.8 g*
- ➤ *Sugar 0.8 g*
- ➤ *Protein 27.2 g*

"The Cheesecake Factory" Southern Fried Catfish

Ingredients

- ➤ 2 eggs
- ➤ 2 tablespoons carbonated water
- ➤ 1 cup pancake mix
- ➤ ½ teaspoon seasoned salt
- ➤ ¼ teaspoon ground black pepper
- ➤ 4 (6-ounce) catfish fillets
- ➤ 1–2 cups canola oil

How to Prepare

1. In a shallow bowl, add eggs and water and beat well.
2. In a separate shallow bowl, add the pancake mix, seasoned salt, and pepper, and mix.
3. Dip the fish fillets in egg mixture, and then coat with seasoned pancake mixture.
4. In a deep skillet, heat the oil over medium-high heat and fry the fish fillets for about 3–4 minutes or until golden-brown on both sides.
5. With a slotted spoon, transfer the fish fillets onto a paper towel-lined plate to drain.
6. Serve hot.

Preparation time: 15 minutes
Cooking time: 4 minutes
Total time: 19 minutes
Servings: 4

Nutritional Values

- *Calories 856*
- *Total Fat 71.9 g*
- *Saturated Fat 7.4 g*
- *Cholesterol 162 mg*
- *Sodium 679 mg*
- *Total Carbs 17.5 g*
- *Fiber 7.5 g*
- *Sugar 0.2 g*
- *Protein 35.2 g*

"The Cheesecake Factory" Fish & Chips

Ingredients

- ➢ 4 cups frozen steak fries
- ➢ 4 (6-ounce) salmon fillets
- ➢ 1–2 tablespoons prepared horseradish
- ➢ 1 tablespoon Parmesan cheese, grated
- ➢ 1 tablespoon Worcestershire sauce

- ➢ 1 teaspoon Dijon mustard
- ➢ Salt, to taste
- ➢ ½ cup panko breadcrumbs
- ➢ Cooking spray

How to Prepare

1. Preheat the oven to 450°F.
2. Arrange a rack in the lower portion of oven.
3. Arrange a second rack in the middle portion of oven.
4. Arrange steak fries onto a baking sheet in a single layer.
5. Place the baking sheet of steak fries onto the lower rack and bake for about 18–20 minutes or until light golden-brown.
6. Meanwhile, place salmon on a foil-lined baking sheet coated with cooking spray.
7. In a small bowl, add the horseradish, cheese, Worcestershire sauce, mustard, and salt, and mix well.
8. Stir in the panko.
9. Coat the salmon fillets with cheese mixture and spray with cooking spray.
10. Arrange the salmon fillets onto a greased baking dish in a single layer.
11. Arrange the baking dish over the middle rack and bake for about 8–10 minutes. or until fish just begins to flake easily with a fork.
12. Serve cod fillets with fries.

Preparation time: 15 minutes
Cooking time: 20 minutes
Total time: 35 minutes
Servings: 4

Nutritional Values
- ➢ *Calories 415*
- ➢ *Total Fat 15.5 g*

- ➢ *Saturated Fat 3 g*
- ➢ *Cholesterol 79 mg*
- ➢ *Sodium 666 mg*
- ➢ *Total Carbs 24.5 g*
- ➢ *Fiber 2.2 g*
- ➢ *Sugar 2.1 g*
- ➢ *Protein 37 g*

"Magnolia Bar and Grill" Crawfish Etouffee

Ingredients

- ➢ 1 pound crawfish tails, cleaned
- ➢ 1 teaspoon salt
- ➢ ¼ teaspoon cayenne pepper

- ➢ ½ cup butter
- ➢ 1 medium onion, chopped finely
- ➢ 1 teaspoon almond flour
- ➢ ¾–1 cup water
- ➢ 1 tablespoon tomato paste
- ➢ 2 thin lemon slices
- ➢ 1 tablespoon scallion, chopped
- ➢ 1 tablespoon fresh parsley, chopped

How to Prepare

1. Season the crawfish tails with salt and cayenne pepper. Set aside.
2. In a pan, melt the butter over medium heat and cook the onion for about 4–5 minutes.
3. Add the flour and stir until well combined.
4. Add the water, tomato paste and lemon slices and cook for about 20 minutes.
5. Stir in the crawfish tails and cook, covered for about 8 minutes.
6. Stir in the scallion and parsley and cook for about 2 minutes.
7. Serve hot.

Preparation time: 15 minutes
Cooking time: 35 minutes
Total time: 50 minutes
Servings: 4

Nutritional Values

- ➢ *Calories 352*
- ➢ *Total Fat 24.7 g*
- ➢ *Saturated Fat 16 g*
- ➢ *Cholesterol 262 mg*
- ➢ *Sodium 830 mg*
- ➢ *Total Carbs 3.7 g*
- ➢ *Fiber 0.9 g*
- ➢ *Sugar 1.7 g*

➢ *Protein 27.6 g*

"Red Lobster" Shrimp Scampi

Ingredients

- ➢ ½ cup plus 1 tablespoon unsalted butter, divided
- ➢ 3 teaspoons garlic, minced
- ➢ 1 cup white wine
- ➢ 1 pound shrimp, peeled and deveined
- ➢ ½ cup Italian breadcrumbs

How to Prepare

1. Preheat the oven to 350°F.
2. In a small saucepan, melt ½ cup of the butter over medium heat and sauté the garlic for about 30 seconds.
3. Stir in the white wine and cook for about 1–2 minutes or until heated through.
4. In a small microwave bowl, add the remaining butter and microwave until melted.
5. Remove from microwave and stir in breadcrumbs until well combined.
6. Place shrimp in a baking dish and top with wine mixture, followed by the buttered breadcrumbs.
7. Bake for about 10–12 minutes.
8. Serve hot.

Preparation time: 15 minutes
Cooking time: 15 minutes
Total time: 30 minutes
Servings: 4

Nutritional Values

- *Calories 626*
- *Total Fat 38.1 g*
- *Saturated Fat 22.9 g*
- *Cholesterol 410 mg*
- *Sodium 750 mg*
- *Total Carbs 18.4 g*
- *Fiber 0.9 g*
- *Sugar 1.8 g*
- *Protein 7.4 g*

"Panda Express" Honey Walnut Shrimp

Ingredients

- ➢ 1 cup water
- ➢ 2/3 cup white sugar
- ➢ ½ cup walnut halves
- ➢ 4 egg whites
- ➢ 2/3 cup cornstarch
- ➢ 1 pound large shrimp, peeled and deveined

➢ ¼ cup mayonnaise
➢ 2 tablespoons honey
➢ 1 tablespoon sweetened condensed milk
➢ 1 cup vegetable oil

How to Prepare

1. In a small saucepan, add the water, sugar, and walnuts, and bring to a boil.
2. Cook for about 2 minutes.
3. Remove the walnuts from heat and place on a dish to dry.
4. In a bowl, add the egg whites and beat until foamy.
5. Add the cornstarch and beat until well combined.
6. Coat the shrimp with cornstarch mixture evenly and let them drip off excess.
7. In a medium pan, heat the oil over medium-high heat and fry for about 4–5 minutes or until light golden-brown.
8. **Sauce:** In a bowl, add the mayonnaise, honey, and condensed milk, and beat until well combined.
9. Add the fried shrimp into the bowl of sauce and gently, stir to combine.
10. Divide the shrimp onto serving plates and serve with the topping of candied walnuts.

Preparation time: 15 minutes
Cooking time: 10 minutes
Total time: 25 minutes
Servings: 4

Nutritional Values

➢ *Calories 997*
➢ *Total Fat 69.1 g*
➢ *Saturated Fat 12.2 g*
➢ *Cholesterol 167 mg*
➢ *Sodium 290 mg*

> ➢ *Total Carbs 71.4 g*
> ➢ *Fiber 1.3 g*
> ➢ *Sugar 45.9 g*
> ➢ *Protein 29.2 g*

"Long Johns Silver's" Seafood Bake

Ingredients

- 12 ounces imitation lobster meat
- 12 ounces imitation crab meat
- 6 ounces shrimp, peeled and deveined
- 1 cup mayonnaise
- 2 tablespoons scallions, sliced green onions
- ½ cup Mozzarella cheese, shredded

How to Prepare

1. Preheat the oven to 350ºF. Grease a baking dish.
2. In a large bowl, add seafood, mayonnaise, and scallion, and stir to combine.
3. Place the seafood mixture into the prepared baking dish evenly and top with Mozzarella cheese.
4. Bake for about 25–30 minutes.
5. Serve hot.

Preparation time: 15 minutes
Cooking time: 30 minutes
Total time: 45 minutes
Servings: 4

Nutritional Values

- *Calories 446*
- *Total Fat 21.7 g*
- *Saturated Fat 3.7 g*
- *Cholesterol 14 mg*
- *Sodium 1,400 mg*
- *Total Carbs 38.8 g*
- *Fiber 1.5 g*
- *Sugar 14.2 g*
- *Protein 25.5 g*

CHAPTER 7
VEGETARIAN RECIPES

"California Pizza Kitchen" Chopped BBQ Tofu Salad

Ingredients
- 1 (16-ounce) package tofu; pressed, drained, and cubed
- 1 cup BBQ sauce, divided
- ½ cup mayonnaise

- ➢ ¼ cup soy milk
- ➢ 1/8 cup fresh parsley, chopped
- ➢ 1 teaspoon garlic powder
- ➢ Salt and ground black pepper, to taste
- ➢ 1 can black beans, drained and rinsed
- ➢ 1 cup corn
- ➢ 8 cups lettuce, chopped
- ➢ 4 medium tomatoes, chopped
- ➢ 2 cups carrots, peeled and shredded
- ➢ 2 avocados; peeled, pitted, and chopped

How to Prepare

1. In a bowl, add tofu cubes and ½ cup of BBQ sauce and toss to coat well.
2. Refrigerate to marinade for at least 20–30 minutes.
3. Preheat the oven to 400°F.
4. Lightly, grease a large baking sheet.
5. Remove the tofu cubes from bowl and place onto the prepared baking sheet in a single layer.
6. Bake for about 15 minutes.
7. Remove the baking sheet from oven and flip the tofu cubes.
8. Coat the tofu cubes with remaining BBQ sauce lightly.
9. Bake for about 10–15 minutes.
10. Remove from the oven and set aside to cool slightly.
11. **Dressing:** In a bowl, add mayonnaise, soy milk, parsley, garlic powder, salt, black pepper and 3 tablespoons of BBQ sauce and beat until well combined.
12. Divide beans, corn, lettuce, tomatoes, carrots, avocado, and tofu onto serving plates.
13. Drizzle with dressing and serve.

Preparation time: 20 minutes
Cooking time: 30 minutes

Total time: 50 minutes
Servings: 6

Nutritional Values

- *Calories 623*
- *Total Fat 24.6 g*
- *Saturated Fat 4.7 g*
- *Cholesterol 5 mg*
- *Sodium 692 mg*
- *Total Carbs 83 g*
- *Fiber 18.7 g*
- *Sugar 20.4 g*
- *Protein 24.6 g*

"Panera Bread" Modern Greek Quinoa Salad

Ingredients

- ➤ 1 cup uncooked quinoa, rinsed
- ➤ 2 cups water
- ➤ 2 cups fresh spinach, torn
- ➤ 3 apples, cored and chopped
- ➤ 5–6 tablespoons fresh orange juice
- ➤ 3 tablespoons olive oil

How to Prepare

1. In a pan, add quinoa and water over medium-high heat and bring to a boil.
2. Reduce the heat to medium-low and cook, covered for about 15–20 minutes, or until all the liquid is absorbed.
3. Remove from the heat and with a fork, fluff the quinoa.
4. Transfer the quinoa into a large bowl and refrigerate, uncovered to chill.
5. In the bowl of quinoa, add spinach, apples, orange juice and oil and stir to combine.
6. Serve immediately.

Preparation time: 15 minutes
Cooking time: 20 minutes
Total time: 35 minutes
Servings: 3

Nutritional Values

➢ *Calories 461*
➢ *Total Fat 18 g*
➢ *Saturated Fat 2.4 g*
➢ *Cholesterol 0 mg*
➢ *Sodium 26 mg*
➢ *Total Carbs 70.6 g*
➢ *Fiber 9.9 g*
➢ *Sugar 25.5 g*
➢ *Protein 9.4 g*

"The Cheesecake Factory"
Santorini Farro Salad

Ingredients

Tzatziki Sauce

- 1 ½ cups Greek plain yogurt
- ½ cup English cucumber, grated
- 2 garlic cloves, minced
- 1 teaspoon fresh dill, chopped
- 1 teaspoon fresh mint, chopped
- Salt, to taste

Salad

- 2 cups cooked farro
- ½ of English cucumber, chopped
- 1 cup cherry tomatoes, halved
- 2 large cooked beets, chopped
- ¼ cup red onion, sliced thinly
- ¼ cup feta cheese, crumbled
- 1 tablespoon balsamic vinegar
- 1 tablespoon extra-virgin olive oil
- Salt and ground black pepper, to taste

How to Prepare

1. **Tzatziki sauce:** In a bowl, place all the ingredients and mix well.
2. Refrigerate to chill before using.
3. **Salad:** Add all ingredients into a large salad bowl and mix.
4. Drizzle with Tzatziki sauce and serve.

Preparation time: 15 minutes
Total time: 15 minutes
Servings: 4

Nutritional Values

- *Calories 476*
- *Total Fat 6.8 g*

- ➢ *Saturated Fat 2.8 g*
- ➢ *Cholesterol 14 mg*
- ➢ *Sodium 309 mg*
- ➢ *Total Carbs 81.1 g*
- ➢ *Fiber 7.5 g*
- ➢ *Sugar 12 g*
- ➢ *Protein 21.9 g*

"P.F. Chang's China Bistro" Vegetarian Lettuce Wraps

Ingredients

- ➤ 3 tablespoons low-sodium soy sauce
- ➤ 3 tablespoons hoisin sauce
- ➤ 2 tablespoons rice vinegar

- ➢ 1 teaspoon sesame oil
- ➢ 2 teaspoons canola oil
- ➢ 1 (14-ounce) package extra-firm tofu; pressed, drained, and crumbled
- ➢ 8 ounces fresh baby Bella mushrooms, chopped finely
- ➢ 1 (8-ounce) can water chestnuts, drained and chopped finely
- ➢ 4 scallions, sliced thinly and divided
- ➢ 2 teaspoons fresh ginger, grated
- ➢ 2 garlic cloves, minced
- ➢ ¼ teaspoon red pepper flakes, crushed
- ➢ 8 large romaine lettuce leaves
- ➢ 1 large carrot, peeled and grated

How to Prepare

1. In a small bowl, add soy sauce, hoisin, vinegar, and sesame oil, and mix well. Set aside.
2. In a large non-stick skillet, heat the canola oil over medium-high heat and cook the tofu for about 5 minutes, stirring frequently.
3. Add the mushrooms and cook for about 3 minutes, stirring frequently.
4. Stir in the water chestnuts, 2 scallions, ginger, garlic, and red pepper flakes, and cook for about 1 minute.
5. Stir in sauce and cook for about 40–60 seconds.
6. Remove the wok from heat and set aside to cool slightly.
7. Arrange the tofu leaves onto serving plates.
8. Place tofu mixture over each lettuce leaf evenly and top with remaining scallions and carrots.
9. Serve immediately.

Preparation time: 15 minutes
Cooking time: 10 minutes
Total time: 25 minutes
Servings: 4

Nutritional Values

- ➢ *Calories 275*
- ➢ *Total Fat 10.2 g*
- ➢ *Saturated Fat 1 g*
- ➢ *Cholesterol 0 mg*
- ➢ *Sodium 889 mg*
- ➢ *Total Carbs 34 g*
- ➢ *Fiber 2.4 g*
- ➢ *Sugar 6.9 g*
- ➢ *Protein 14.7 g*

"Chipotle Mexican Grill" Sofritas Burrito Bowl

Ingredients

<u>Sofritas</u>

- ➤ 2 poblano peppers
- ➤ ½ cup vegetable broth
- ➤ 4 chiles from a can of chipotles in adobo sauce
- ➤ 2 tablespoons adobo sauce

- ➤ 2 tablespoons tomato paste
- ➤ 2 garlic cloves, minced
- ➤ 1 teaspoon ancho chili powder
- ➤ ½ teaspoon dried oregano, crushed
- ➤ ½ teaspoon ground cumin
- ➤ ½ teaspoon sea salt
- ➤ ½ teaspoon ground black pepper
- ➤ 1 teaspoon vegetable oil
- ➤ 16 ounces extra-firm tofu; pressed, drained, and crumbled

<u>Burrito Bowl</u>
- ➤ 2 cups cooked brown rice
- ➤ 1 ½ cups cooked black beans
- ➤ ½ cup fresh corn kernels
- ➤ 4 cups romaine lettuce, shredded
- ➤ 2 avocados; peeled, pitted, and chopped
- ➤ 1 cup salsa
- ➤ ½ cup cashew cheese sauce
- ➤ 2 tablespoons fresh cilantro, chopped

How to Prepare

1. Preheat the broiler of oven.
2. **Sofritas:** Arrange the poblano peppers onto a baking sheet and place broil for about 3–5 minutes per side, or until charred.
3. Remove the poblano peppers from oven and set aside to cool.
4. After cooling, peel off the outer skin of peppers and then remove the seeds.
5. In a food processor, add the peppers and remaining ingredients (except for oil and tofu) and pulse until smooth in a large non-stick wok, heat oil over medium-high heat. Cook the tofu and sauce for about 10 minutes, stirring frequently.
6. Remove the wok from heat.
7. Divide the sofritos, rice, black beans, corn kernels, lettuce, and avocados into serving bowls.
8. Top with the salsa, cheese sauce, and cilantro, and serve.

Preparation time: 20 minutes
Cooking time: 20 minutes
Total time: 40 minutes
Servings: 4

Nutritional Values

- Calories 908
- Total Fat 35 g
- Saturated Fat 6.4 g
- Cholesterol 0 mg
- Sodium 202 mg
- Total Carbs 126 g
- Fiber 22.6 g
- Sugar 11.8 g
- Protein 33.1 g

"Panda Express" Super Greens

Ingredients

- ➢ 2 tablespoons avocado oil
- ➢ 1–2 cloves garlic, minced
- ➢ ½ teaspoon ground ginger
- ➢ ¼ teaspoon red pepper flakes, crushed
- ➢ 6 tablespoons water
- ➢ 2 tablespoons soy sauce
- ➢ 4 cups broccoli floret
- ➢ 4 cups green cabbage, chopped roughly
- ➢ 6 cups fresh kale, tough ribs removed and chopped roughly

How to Prepare

1. In a large wok, heat oil over medium-high heat and sauté the garlic, ground ginger, and red pepper flakes for about 1 minute.
2. Add the soy sauce and water and stir to combine.
3. In the wok, place broccoli and top with cabbage, followed by the kale.
4. Cover the wok and cook for about 3–4 minutes.
5. Stir the vegetables to combine and remove from the heat.
6. Serve warm.

Preparation time: 15 minutes
Cooking time: 6 minutes
Total time: 21 minutes
Servings: 3

Nutritional Values
- *Calories 152*
- *Total Fat 1.7 g*
- *Saturated Fat 0.3 g*
- *Cholesterol 0 mg*
- *Sodium 718 mg*
- *Total Carbs 29.4 g*
- *Fiber 8.1 g*
- *Sugar 5.3 g*
- *Protein 9.5 g*

"The Cheesecake Factory" Eggplant Parmesan

Ingredients

- ➢ 3 large eggs, beaten
- ➢ 2½ cups panko breadcrumbs
- ➢ 3 medium eggplants, cut into ¼-inch slices
- ➢ 2 (4 ½-ounces) jars sliced mushrooms, drained

- ➢ ½ teaspoon dried basil
- ➢ 1/8 teaspoon dried oregano
- ➢ 2 cups mozzarella cheese, shredded
- ➢ ½ cup Parmesan cheese, shredded
- ➢ 1 (28-ounce) jar spaghetti sauce

How to Prepare

1. Preheat the oven to 350°F.
2. Grease 2 baking sheets.
3. Place eggs and breadcrumbs respectively in 2 different shallow bowls.
4. Dip the eggplant slices in eggs and then coat with breadcrumbs.
5. Arrange the eggplant slices onto the prepared baking sheets in a single layer.
6. Bake for about 15–20 minutes, or until golden-brown, flipping once halfway through.
7. Again, set the temperature of oven to 350°F.
8. In a small bowl, add mushrooms and dried herbs and mix.
9. In a separate small bowl, mix together both cheeses.
10. In the bottom of a greased 13 x 9-inch baking dish, place ½ cup of spaghetti sauce evenly.
11. Place about 1/3 of the mushroom mixture over sauce, followed by 1/3 of the eggplant slices, ¾ cup of sauce, and 1/3 of the cheese mixture.
12. Repeat the layers twice.
13. Bake for about 25–30 minutes, or until cheese is melted.
14. Serve warm.

Preparation time: 20 minutes
Cooking time: 50 minutes
Total time: 1 hour, 10 minutes
Servings: 8

Nutritional Values

➢ Calories 152
➢ Total Fat 1.7 g
➢ Saturated Fat 0.3 g
➢ Cholesterol 0 mg
➢ Sodium 718 mg
➢ Total Carbs 29.4 g
➢ Fiber 8.1 g
➢ Sugar 5.3 g
➢ Protein 9.5 g

"Hash Barrel" Hash Brown Casserole

Ingredients

- 10 ¾ ounces condensed cream of chicken soup
- 8 ounces sour cream
- 4 ounces butter, melted
- ½ cup onion, minced
- 2 pounds hash browns
- Salt and ground black pepper, to taste
- 2 cups cheddar cheese, shredded

How to Prepare

1. Preheat the oven to 350ºF.
2. Grease a 9 x 13-inch baking dish.
3. In a medium bowl, add the chicken soup, sour cream, butter, and onion, and mix well.
4. In the bottom of the prepared baking dish, spread the potatoes and season with salt and black pepper.
5. Top with butter mixture and finally sprinkle with cheese.
6. Bake for about 45 minutes, or until cheese is bubbly.
7. Serve warm.

Preparation time: 15 minutes
Cooking time: 45 minutes
Total time: 1 hour
Servings: 6

Nutritional Values

➢ *Calories 802*
➢ *Total Fat 55.7 g*
➢ *Saturated Fat 25.9 g*
➢ *Cholesterol 99 mg*
➢ *Sodium 1,111 mg*
➢ *Total Carbs 60.3 g*
➢ *Fiber 5.5 g*
➢ *Sugar 3.4 g*
➢ *Protein 16.2 g*

"Olive Garden" Gnocchi with Spicy Tomato & Wine Sauce

Ingredients

- ➢ 2 tablespoons extra-virgin olive oil
- ➢ 6 garlic cloves
- ➢ ½ teaspoon chili flakes

- ➢ 1 cup chicken broth
- ➢ 1 cup dry white wine
- ➢ 2 (14 ½-ounce) cans diced tomatoes
- ➢ ¼ cup fresh basil, chopped
- ➢ ½ cup Parmesan cheese, grated
- ➢ ¼ cup chilled butter, cut into 1-inch cubes
- ➢ Salt and ground black pepper, to taste
- ➢ 1 pound gnocchi

How to Prepare

1. In a pan, add the oil, garlic, and chili flakes over medium heat, and cook for about 2 minutes.
2. Add the broth and wine and simmer for about 10 minutes.
3. Stir in the tomatoes and basil and simmer for about 30 minutes.
4. Remove from the heat and stir in the Parmesan cheese, butter, salt, and black pepper.
5. With an immersion blender, blend the sauce until smooth.
6. Meanwhile, in a pan of salted boiling water, cook the gnocchi for about 3 minutes.
7. With a slotted spoon, transfer the gnocchi into the pan of sauce.
8. With a wooden spoon gently, mix the gnocchi with sauce and serve.

Preparation time: 15 minutes
Cooking time: 40 minutes
Total time: 55 minutes
Servings: 6

Nutritional Values

- ➢ *Calories 314*
- ➢ *Total Fat 14.9 g*
- ➢ *Saturated Fat 6.4 g*
- ➢ *Cholesterol 26 mg*
- ➢ *Sodium 928 mg*
- ➢ *Total Carbs 30.5 g*

> *Fiber 3 g*
> *Sugar 3.5 g*
> *Protein 7.4 g*

"Panda Express" Fried Rice

Ingredients

- ➢ 2 tablespoons extra-virgin olive oil
- ➢ ½ cup white onion, chopped
- ➢ ½ cup carrot, peeled and cut into small pieces
- ➢ 4 ounces tofu; pressed, drained, and crumbled
- ➢ 1 teaspoon garlic powder
- ➢ ½ teaspoon ground turmeric
- ➢ ½ teaspoon salt
- ➢ 1/8 teaspoon ground black pepper

- ➢ 2 cups cooked rice
- ➢ ½ cup fresh peas, shelled
- ➢ 2 tablespoons tamari
- ➢ ½ teaspoon sesame oil

How to Prepare

1. In a wok, heat 1 tablespoon of the olive oil over medium-high heat and cook the onions and carrots for about 5 minutes, stirring frequently.
2. With a slotted spoon, transfer the carrot mixture into a bowl.
3. In the same wok, heat the remaining oil over medium-high heat and cook the tofu, turmeric, garlic powder, salt, and black pepper for about 5 minutes, stirring frequently.
4. Add the cooked rice, carrot mixture, and peas, and cook for about 1 minute.
5. Add the tamari and sesame oil and cook for about 5 minutes, stirring frequently.
6. Serve hot.

Preparation time: 15 minutes
Cooking time: 16 minutes
Total time: 31 minutes
Servings: 4

Nutritional Values

- ➢ *Calories 457*
- ➢ *Total Fat 9.5 g*
- ➢ *Saturated Fat 1.5 g*
- ➢ *Cholesterol 0 mg*
- ➢ *Sodium 813 mg*
- ➢ *Total Carbs 81 g*
- ➢ *Fiber 3.3 g*
- ➢ *Sugar 2.9 g*
- ➢ *Protein 11.3 g*

CHAPTER 8
BURGER RECIPES

"In-N-Out Burger" Burgers

Ingredients
- 2 tablespoons vegetable oil
- 2 large onions, chopped finely
- Salt, to taste
- ½ cup water
- ¼ cup mayonnaise
- 2 tablespoons ketchup

- ➢ 1 tablespoon sweet pickle relish
- ➢ ½ teaspoon white vinegar
- ➢ 2 pounds 60% ground chuck
- ➢ Ground black pepper, to taste
- ➢ 1 ½ teaspoons mustard
- ➢ 8 American cheese slices
- ➢ 4 hamburger buns, toasted
- ➢ 1 cup iceberg lettuce, shredded
- ➢ 4–8 tomato slices

How to Prepare

1. Heat oil in pan over medium heat and stir in the onions.
2. Cover the pan and cook for about 30 minutes, stirring occasionally.
3. Uncover the pan and cook for about 5 minutes.
4. Stir in water and cook for about 4–5 minutes or until all the liquid is absorbed.
5. In a bowl, add beef, salt, and black pepper, and mix well.
6. Make 8 (½-inch thick) patties from beef.
7. Heat a lightly greased griddle over medium heat and cook the patties for about 3–5 minutes.
8. Spread mustard on top of each patty and flip them.
9. Top each patty with 1 chase slice and cook for about 3–4 minutes or until desired doneness.
10. Spread 1 tablespoon of mayonnaise mixture over the bottom half of each bun and top with lettuce and tomato slices.
11. Place 1 patty over each bun and top with caramelized onion.
12. Cover with top half of bun and serve.

Preparation time: 20 minutes
Cooking time: 50 minutes
Total time: 1 hour 10 minutes
Servings: 8

Nutritional Values

- Calories 428
- Total Fat 19.5 g
- Saturated Fat 6.9 g
- Cholesterol 120 mg
- Sodium 596 mg
- Total Carbs 20.4 g
- Fiber 1.1 g
- Sugar 5.5 g
- Protein 41.2 g

"The Cheesecake Factory" American Burger

Ingredients

- 1 pound ground beef
- 1 large egg, lightly beaten
- ½ cup seasoned breadcrumbs
- Salt and ground black pepper, to taste
- 1 tablespoon olive oil

> ➤ 4 sesame seed hamburger buns, split

How to Prepare

1. Preheat the grill to medium heat.
2. Grease the grill grate.
3. In a large bowl, add the beef, egg, breadcrumbs, salt, and black pepper, and mix until well combined.
4. Make 4 (½-inch thick) patties from the mixture.
5. With your thumb, press a shallow indentation in the center of each patty.
6. Brush both sides of each patty with oil.
7. Place the burgers onto the grill and cook, covered for about 4–5 minutes per side.
8. Serve patties onto buns with your favorite toppings.

Preparation time: 15 minutes
Cooking time: 10 minutes
Total time: 25 minutes
Servings: 4

Nutritional Values

- ➤ *Calories 437*
- ➤ *Total Fat 15.6 g*
- ➤ *Saturated Fat 3.6 g*
- ➤ *Cholesterol 148 mg*
- ➤ *Sodium 547 mg*
- ➤ *Total Carbs 30.6 g*
- ➤ *Fiber 0.5 g*
- ➤ *Sugar 0.1 g*
- ➤ *Protein 41.5 g*

"Red Robin" Banzai Burger

Ingredients

- 1 1/3 pounds ground beef
- 2 cups teriyaki sauce, divided
- 4 cheddar cheese slices
- 4 pineapple rings
- 4 hamburger buns
- 4 tablespoons mayonnaise
- 4 tomato slices

➢ 1 cup lettuce, shredded

How to Prepare

1. Make 4 equal-sized patties from beef.
2. In a bowl, place the patties and 1 cup of teriyaki sauce and refrigerate to marinate for at least 30 minutes.
3. In another bowl, place the remaining teriyaki sauce and pineapple rings and mix until well combined.
4. Set aside for at least 30 minutes.
5. Preheat the grill to high heat.
6. Grease the grill grate.
7. Remove the patties from teriyaki sauce.
8. Place the patties onto the grill and cook for about 3–5 minutes per side, or until desired doneness.
9. In the last minute of cooking, place 1 cheese slice on top of each patty.
10. Place the pineapple rings onto the grill over medium heat and cook for about 1 minute per side.
11. Spread ½ tablespoon of mayonnaise on each half of each hamburger bun.
12. Place tomato slices on each bottom bun and top with patties, followed by pineapple rings and lettuce.
13. Cover each with top half and serve.

Preparation time: 15 minutes
Cooking time: 12 minutes
Total time: 27 minutes
Servings: 4

Nutritional Values

➢ *Calories 722*
➢ *Total Fat 24.8 g*
➢ *Saturated Fat 9.6 g*

➢ *Cholesterol 169 mg*
➢ *Sodium 900 mg*
➢ *Total Carbs 55.1 g*
➢ *Fiber 3.5 g*
➢ *Sugar 26.7 g*
➢ *Protein 68.4 g*

"McDonald's" McRib

Ingredients

Dry Rub

- ¼ cup brown sugar
- 1/3 cup kosher salt
- 2 tablespoons red chili powder
- 2 tablespoons ground black pepper
- 1 tablespoon ground cumin
- 1 teaspoon cayenne pepper

Burgers

- ➤ 2 racks baby back pork ribs
- ➤ 1 cup barbecue sauce, divided
- ➤ 4 sesame hamburger rolls, split and toasted
- ➤ 1 cup coleslaw

How to Prepare

1. Preheat the oven to 325°F. Line a baking sheet with a piece of foil.
2. **Dry rub:** In a bowl, mix together all ingredients.
3. Season the ribs with some of spice rub generously.
4. Place the ribs over the foil, arranged in the baking sheet.
5. Arrange a parchment paper over ribs and then, wrap foil over the edges.
6. With a large piece of foil, cover the baking sheet and bake for about 2 ¾ hours.
7. Remove the baking sheet from oven and carefully, unwrap the ribs.
8. Pull out the bones, stuffing any loose pieces of meat back into the holes.
9. With a piece of foil, cover the ribs and refrigerate overnight.
10. Remove the foil and cut each rack in half.
11. Preheat a charcoal grill for high heat.
12. Lightly, grease the grill grate.
13. Brush both sides of ribs with barbecue sauce generously.
14. Place the ribs onto grill and cook for about 3–4 minutes per side.
15. Remove from grill and brush the ribs with some sauce.
16. Place some barbecue sauce each roll and top with rib sections and coleslaw.
17. Serve immediately.

Preparation time: 15 minutes
Cooking time: 2 hours, 53 minutes
Total time: 3 hours, 8 minutes
Servings: 4

Nutritional Values

- Calories 976
- Total Fat 45.1 g
- Saturated Fat 14.3 g
- Cholesterol 352 mg
- Sodium 1,202 mg
- Total Carbs 67.8 g
- Fiber 5.8 g
- Sugar 29.5 g
- Protein 74.9 g

"Nando's" Peri Peri Chicken Burger

Ingredients

<u>Peri Peri Sauce</u>

- ➤ 2 birds-eye red chilies
- ➤ 1 large red bell pepper, seeded and cut into chunks
- ➤ 5 garlic cloves, peeled
- ➤ 3 tablespoons vegetable oil
- ➤ 4 tablespoons malt vinegar
- ➤ 2 tablespoons paprika

- ➤ 1 tablespoon dried oregano
- ➤ 2 teaspoons onion powder
- ➤ 1 ½ teaspoons white sugar
- ➤ Salt and ground black pepper, to taste

Pink Sauce
- ➤ 3 tablespoons peri peri sauce
- ➤ ½ cup mayonnaise
- ➤ ¼ cup sour cream

Burgers
- ➤ 1 tablespoon olive oil
- ➤ 4 (4-ounce) skinless, boneless chicken thigh fillets
- ➤ 4 soft rolls
- ➤ 2 tomatoes, sliced
- ➤ 4 lettuce leaves

How to Prepare

1. **Peri peri sauce:** In a food processor, add all ingredients and pulse until smooth.
2. In a Ziplock bag, place ½ cup of peri peri sauce and chicken.
3. Seal the bag and shake to coat well.
4. Refrigerate to marinate for at least 3 hours.
5. **Pink sauce:** In a bowl, place all the ingredients with 3 tablespoons of peri peri sauce and mix well. Set aside.
6. Meanwhile, heat oil in a fry pan over medium-high heat and cook the chicken breasts for about 4–5 minutes per side or until cooked through.
7. Place lettuce over bottom half of each bun and top with tomato, chicken, and pink sauce.
8. Cover with top half of buns and serve.

Preparation time: 20 minutes
Cooking time: 10 minutes

Total time: 30 minutes
Servings: 4

Nutritional Values

- *Calories 874*
- *Total Fat 42.3 g*
- *Saturated Fat 10 g*
- *Cholesterol 110 mg*
- *Sodium 900 mg*
- *Total Carbs 87.7 g*
- *Fiber 5.1 g*
- *Sugar 20.5 g*
- *Protein 38.8 g*

"McDonald's" Hamburger

Ingredients

- ➤ 1 teaspoon dried onion flakes
- ➤ 4 teaspoons boiling water
- ➤ ¼ pound ground beef
- ➤ 2 plain hamburgers buns
- ➤ Salt, to taste
- ➤ 2 tablespoons ketchup
- ➤ 1 teaspoon prepared mustard
- ➤ 2 dill pickle slices

How to Prepare

1. In a bowl, place the dried onion and boiling water and set aside until rehydrated and no longer dry and crunchy.
2. Make 2 (1/8-inch-thick) patties from ground beef.
3. Heat a cast iron skillet over medium heat and cook the patties for about 2 minutes per side, sprinkling with the salt lightly during cooking.
4. Spread the ketchup over top half of each bun, followed by mustard, onion, and top with the pickle slice.
5. Place 1 beef patty on the bottom half of each bun and immediately, cover with top halves.
6. Arrange the burgers onto a microwave-safe plate and microwave for about 10–15 seconds.
7. Serve immediately.

Preparation time: 10 minutes
Cooking time: 5 minutes
Total time: 15 minutes
Servings: 2

Nutritional Values

- *Calories 235*
- *Total Fat 5.2 g*
- *Saturated Fat 1.4 g*
- *Cholesterol 51 mg*
- *Sodium 605 mg*
- *Total Carbs 25.8 g*
- *Fiber 1.3 g*
- *Sugar 6.8 g*
- *Protein 20.7 g*

"KFC" Zinger Burger

Ingredients

- ➤ 3 (6-ounce) boneless, skinless chicken breasts
- ➤ 2 tablespoons Worcestershire sauce
- ➤ 1 teaspoon mustard powder
- ➤ Salt and ground black pepper, to taste
- ➤ 2 tablespoons flour
- ➤ 1 egg
- ➤ 2 tablespoons water

- ➢ 1 ½ cups breadcrumbs
- ➢ 6 soft seeded burger buns, halved and toasted
- ➢ 2–3 cups olive oil
- ➢ 1/3 cup mayonnaise
- ➢ 1–2 cups crispy lettuce, shredded

How to Prepare

1. In a bowl, add the chicken breasts, Worcestershire sauce, mustard, salt, and black pepper, and mix well.
2. Refrigerate to marinate for about 4 hours.
3. In a shallow bowl, place the flour.
4. In a second shallow bowl, place the egg and water and beat well.
5. In a third shallow bowl, place the breadcrumbs.
6. Coat the chicken breasts with flour, then dip in to the egg and finally coat with breadcrumbs.
7. In a large skillet, heat the oil over medium-high heat and cook the coated chicken breasts for about 12–15 minutes or until golden-brown and crispy, flipping occasionally.
8. Spread the mayonnaise over bottom half of each bun and top with lettuce, followed by 1 patty.
9. Cover with top half of bun and serve.

Preparation time: 20 minutes
Cooking time: 15 minutes
Total time: 35 minutes
Servings: 6

Nutritional Values

- ➢ *Calories 1,200*
- ➢ *Total Fat 99 g*
- ➢ *Saturated Fat 116 g*
- ➢ *Cholesterol 15.9 mg*
- ➢ *Sodium 894 mg*
- ➢ *Total Carbs 49.9 g*

> *Fiber 4.4 g*
> *Sugar 6.9 g*
> *Protein 36.6 g*

"Wendy's" Bacon Portobella Mushroom Melt

Ingredients

Burgers

- ➤ 14 ounces lean ground beef
- ➤ 1 teaspoon seasoning salt
- ➤ 2 tablespoons butter, divided
- ➤ 6 cremini mushrooms, sliced
- ➤ Salt and ground black pepper, to taste
- ➤ 6 cooked smoked bacon strips

➢ 4 cheddar cheese slices
➢ 2 brioche buns, toasted

Cheese Sauce
➢ 2 tablespoons butter
➢ 2 tablespoons flour
➢ 1 cup milk
➢ 1 cup aged cheddar cheese, grated
➢ Salt, to taste
➢ Pinch of cayenne pepper

How to Prepare

1. In a bowl, add the beef and seasoning salt and mix well.
2. Make 2 equal-sized patties from beef. Set aside.
3. In a small frying pan, melt 1 tablespoon of butter over medium heat and sauté the mushrooms with salt and black pepper for about 6–7 minutes.
4. Remove from the heat and set aside.
5. **Sauce:** In another frying pan, melt the butter over medium-low heat.
6. Stir in the flour and cook for about 1 minute.
7. Slowly add in the milk, beating continuously and bring to a gentle simmer.
8. Add the cheese, salt, and cayenne, and stir until cheese is melted.
9. Set aside, covered to keep warm.
10. Heat a cast iron pan over medium heat and cook the patties for about 4–6 min per side.
11. Remove from the heat and set aside.
12. Spread the remaining butter over buns.
13. Place 1 cheese slice on the bottom of each bun and top with the patty, followed by the second cheese slice, bacon, cheese sauce, and mushrooms.
14. Cover with the top of the bun and serve.

Preparation time: 15 minutes
Cooking time: 19 minutes
Total time: 34 minutes
Servings: 2

Nutritional Values

- *Calories 1,300*
- *Total Fat 88.2 g*
- *Saturated Fat 45.5 g*
- *Cholesterol 392 mg*
- *Sodium 1,000 mg*
- *Total Carbs 42.6 g*
- *Fiber 3.8 g*
- *Sugar 10 g*
- *Protein 100 g*

"Huston's Restaurant" Veggie Burgers

Ingredients

- ➢ 4 tablespoons hickory barbecue sauce
- ➢ 1 tablespoon molasses
- ➢ 1 (15-ounce) can black beans, drained
- ➢ 2 cups cooked brown rice
- ➢ 1 tablespoon oat bran

- ➢ 2 tablespoons onions, chopped finely
- ➢ 1 tablespoon canned beets, chopped finely
- ➢ 1 teaspoon beet juice
- ➢ 1 teaspoon red chili powder
- ➢ ¼ teaspoon ground cumin
- ➢ ¼ teaspoon ground black pepper
- ➢ Kosher salt, to taste
- ➢ 1 tablespoon pickled jalapeño pepper, chopped finely
- ➢ 1 egg white
- ➢ 2 teaspoons olive oil
- ➢ 4 Monterey Jack cheese slices
- ➢ 4 burger buns, toasted
- ➢ 1 tomato, sliced
- ➢ 1 cup fresh baby arugula

How to Prepare

1. In a bowl, mix together barbecue sauce and molasses. Set aside.
2. In a large bowl, place beans and with a fork, mash them.
3. Add 3 tablespoons of barbecue sauce mixture and remaining ingredients except for oil and cheese and mix until well combined.
4. Make 4 (6-ounce) patties from the mixture.
5. In a cast iron wok, heat the oil over medium heat and cook the burgers for about 2 minutes per side.
6. Flip the burgers and coat each with remaining barbecue sauce mixture.
7. Place 1 cheese slice over each burger and cook for about 2 minutes or until cheese is melted.
8. Serve patties onto buns with the toppings of tomato and arugula.

Preparation time: 15 minutes
Cooking time: 6 minutes
Total time: 21 minutes
Servings: 4

Nutritional Values

- Calories 565
- Total Fat 13.6 g
- Saturated Fat 5.9 g
- Cholesterol 25 mg
- Sodium 678 mg
- Total Carbs 86.3 g
- Fiber 14 g
- Sugar 12.1 g
- Protein 27 g

"The Cheesecake Factory" Veggie Burger

Ingredients

- ➢ 1 tablespoon olive oil
- ➢ 1 large onion, chopped finely
- ➢ 4 garlic cloves, minced
- ➢ 1 medium carrot, peeled and shredded
- ➢ 2 teaspoons chili powder

- ➢ 1 teaspoon ground cumin
- ➢ Ground black pepper, to taste
- ➢ 1 (15-ounce) can pinto beans, rinsed and drained
- ➢ 1 (15-ounce) can black beans, rinsed and drained
- ➢ 1 ½ cups quick-cooking oats
- ➢ 2 tablespoons low-sodium soy sauce
- ➢ 2 tablespoons Dijon mustard
- ➢ 1 tablespoon ketchup
- ➢ 8 whole-wheat hamburger buns, split
- ➢ 8 lettuce leaves
- ➢ ½ cup salsa

How to Prepare

1. Preheat the grill to medium heat.
2. Grease the grill grate.
3. In a large nonstick skillet, heat oil over medium-high heat and sauté the onion for about 2 minutes.
4. Add the garlic and sauté for about 1 minute.
5. Stir in carrot and spices and cook for about 2–3 minutes, stirring frequently.
6. Remove from heat and set aside.
7. In a large bowl, add both cans of beans and with a potato masher, mash slightly.
8. Add the carrot mixture, oats, soy sauce, mustard, and ketchup, and mix until well combined.
9. Make 8 (3 ½-inch) patties from the mixture.
10. Place the patties onto the grill and cook, covered for about 4–5 minutes per side or until desired doneness.
11. Serve patties onto buns with the topping of lettuce and salsa.

Preparation time: 20 minutes
Cooking time: 16 minutes
Total time: 36 minutes

Servings: 8

Nutritional Values

- *Calories 453*
- *Total Fat 6 g*
- *Saturated Fat 1 g*
- *Cholesterol 0 mg*
- *Sodium 655 mg*
- *Total Carbs 81.5 g*
- *Fiber 18.4 g*
- *Sugar 7 g*
- *Protein 22.6 g*

CHAPTER 9

PASTA RECIPES

"Pizza Hut" Cavatini

Ingredients

- ➢ 16 ounces mixed pasta (shells, spirals, ziti, and wheels)
- ➢ 1 tablespoon olive oil
- ➢ 1 green bell pepper, seeded and chopped
- ➢ 1 medium white onion, chopped

- ➤ 1 garlic clove, minced
- ➤ ½ pound Italian sausage
- ➤ 2 (16-ounce) jars tomato sauce
- ➤ ¼ pound pepperoni
- ➤ 8 ounces mozzarella cheese, shredded

How to Prepare

1. Preheat the oven to 350°F.
2. In a large pan of lightly salted, boiling water, add pasta, and cook for about 8–10 minutes or according to package's instructions.
3. Meanwhile, heat the oil in a skillet over medium-high heat and sauté the bell pepper, onion, and garlic for about 4–5 minutes.
4. Remove the bell pepper mixture from heat and set aside.
5. Heat another skillet over medium-high heat and cook the sausage for about 7–10 minutes or until browned.
6. With a slotted spoon, place the sausage meat onto a paper towel-lined plate to drain the excess grease.
7. In a large bowl, add sausage meat and tomato sauce and mix well.
8. In the bottom of prepared baking dish, spread a thin layer of sausage mixture.
9. Place half of the pasta over sausage mixture, followed by half of the bell pepper mixture, half of the pepperoni, half of sausage mixture.
10. Repeat these layers once and top with cheese evenly.
11. Bake for about 35–45 minutes or until the cheese is melted.
12. Serve warm.

Preparation time: 20 minutes
Cooking time: 1 hour, 5 minutes
Total time: 1 hour, 25 minutes
Servings: 3

Nutritional Values
- ➤ *Calories 617*

- ➢ *Total Fat 30.1 g*
- ➢ *Saturated Fat 10.9 g*
- ➢ *Cholesterol 127 mg*
- ➢ *Sodium 1,500 mg*
- ➢ *Total Carbs 54.2 g*
- ➢ *Fiber 2.9 g*
- ➢ *Sugar 8.2 g*
- ➢ *Protein 33.3 g*

"Olive Garden" Spaghetti with Meatballs

Ingredients

Sauce

- ➢ 2 tablespoons olive oil
- ➢ 1 ½ cups onions, chopped
- ➢ 3 garlic cloves, minced
- ➢ 2 (12-ounce) cans tomato paste
- ➢ 1 (29-ounce) can tomato sauce

- ➢ 1/3 cup fresh parsley, minced
- ➢ 1 tablespoon dried basil
- ➢ Salt and ground black pepper, to taste
- ➢ 3 cups water

Meatballs

- ➢ 3 pounds ground beef
- ➢ 4 large eggs, lightly beaten
- ➢ 2 cups soft bread, cut into ¼-inch pieces
- ➢ 1 ½ cups whole milk
- ➢ 1 cup Parmesan cheese, grated
- ➢ 3 garlic cloves, minced
- ➢ Salt and ground black pepper, to taste
- ➢ 2 tablespoons canola oil

Spaghetti

- ➢ 2 pounds cooked hot spaghetti

How to Prepare

1. **Sauce:** In a Dutch oven, heat the oil over medium heat and sauté the onion for about 4–5 minutes.
2. Add the garlic and sauté for about 1 minute.
3. Stir in the tomato paste and cook for about 3–5 minutes.
4. Stir in the remaining ingredients and bring to a boil.
5. Reduce heat to low and simmer, covered for about 50 minutes.
6. **Meatballs:** In a bowl, add all the ingredients (except for oil) and mix until well combined.
7. Make about 1 ½-inch balls from the mixture.
8. In a large skillet, heat the oil over medium heat and cook the meatballs in 3 batches for about 4–5 minutes, or until browned.
9. With a slotted spoon, transfer the meatballs onto a paper towel-lined plate to drain.
10. Add the meatballs into the sauce and bring to a boil over medium-high heat.

11. Reduce the heat to low and simmer, covered for about 1 hour, stirring occasionally.
12. Divide the spaghetti onto serving plates and top with meatballs sauce.
13. Serve immediately.

Preparation time: 15 minutes
Cooking time: 2 hours, 5 minutes
Total time: 2 hours, 20 minutes
Servings: 16

Nutritional Values

➤ *Calories 466*
➤ *Total Fat 13.7 g*
➤ *Saturated Fat 4.1 g*
➤ *Cholesterol 170 mg*
➤ *Sodium 482 mg*
➤ *Total Carbs 46.5 g*
➤ *Fiber 2.9 g*
➤ *Sugar 9.3 g*
➤ *Protein 39.6 g*

"Olive Garden" Braised Beef & Tortellini

Ingredients

- ➢ 1 ½ pounds boneless beef short rib
- ➢ ¼ cup flour
- ➢ 3 tablespoons olive oil
- ➢ 1 garlic clove, minced

- ➤ 6 ounces fresh mushrooms, sliced
- ➤ 1 tomato, chopped
- ➤ 8 ounces Marsala wine
- ➤ 1 tablespoon Italian seasoning
- ➤ 1 pound cooked Asiago-filled tortellini

How to Prepare

1. Coat the short ribs with flour evenly.
2. In a large non-stick pan, heat the oil over high heat and sear the short ribs for about 4–5 minutes.
3. Reduce the heat to low.
4. Add the garlic and cook for about 1 minute.
5. Add the mushrooms, tomato, wine, and Italian seasoning, and cook for about 3–4 minutes, stirring continuously.
6. Reduce the heat to low and simmer, covered for about 3 hours, stirring after every 30 minutes.
7. Divide the tortellini onto serving plates and top with beef mixture.
8. Serve immediately.

Preparation time: 15 minutes
Cooking time: 3 hours, 10 minutes
Total time: 3 hours, 25 minutes
Servings: 4

Nutritional Values

- ➤ *Calories 859*
- ➤ *Total Fat 2 g*
- ➤ *Saturated Fat 8.9 g*
- ➤ *Cholesterol 197 mg*
- ➤ *Sodium 611 mg*
- ➤ *Total Carbs 59.3 g*
- ➤ *Fiber 5.1 g*
- ➤ *Sugar 5 g*
- ➤ *Protein 71.1 g*

"California Pizza Kitchen" Chicken Tequila Fettuccine

Ingredients

- ➢ 1 pound dry spinach fettuccine
- ➢ 3 tablespoons unsalted butter, divided
- ➢ ½ cup fresh cilantro, chopped and divided

- ➤ 2 tablespoons jalapeño pepper, seeded and minced
- ➤ 2 tablespoons garlic, minced
- ➤ ½ cup chicken broth
- ➤ 2 tablespoons fresh lime juice
- ➤ 2 tablespoons tequila
- ➤ 1 ½ pounds chicken breast, cut into ¾-inch pieces
- ➤ 3 tablespoons soy sauce
- ➤ ½ cup green bell pepper, seeded and sliced thinly
- ➤ ½ cup yellow bell pepper, seeded and sliced thinly
- ➤ ½ cup red bell pepper, seeded and sliced thinly
- ➤ ¼ cup red onion, sliced thinly
- ➤ 1½ cups heavy cream
- ➤ ½ cup corn tortilla strips

How to Prepare

1. In a large pan of lightly salted boiling water, cook the pasta for about 8–10 minutes or according to package's directions.
2. Drain the pasta well and set aside.
3. In a wok, melt 2 tablespoons of butter over medium heat and cook 1/3 cup of cilantro, jalapeño pepper, and garlic for about 4–5 minutes.
4. Add broth, lime juice and tequila and bring to a boil.
5. Cook for about 2–3 minutes or until thickened, stirring frequently.
6. Remove from the heat and set aside.
7. Meanwhile, in a bowl add chicken and soy sauce and mix well.
8. Set aside for about 5 minutes.
9. In another large wok, melt remaining butter over medium heat and cook the bell peppers and onion for about 3–4 minutes, stirring occasionally.
10. Stir in the chicken, cream, and tequila paste, and bring to a gentle simmer, stirring frequently.
11. Cook for about 3–4 minutes.
12. Add the pasta and toss to coat well.

13. Serve hot with the topping of tortilla strips and remaining cilantro.

Preparation time: 15 minutes
Cooking time: 40 minutes
Total time: 55 minutes
Servings: 6

Nutritional Values

- *Calories 821*
- *Total Fat 51.3 g*
- *Saturated Fat 29.3 g*
- *Cholesterol 294 mg*
- *Sodium 677 mg*
- *Total Carbs 50.7 g*
- *Fiber 0.7 g*
- *Sugar 2.1 g*
- *Protein 36.7 g*

"Chick-fil-A" Mac n' Cheese

Ingredients

- 16 ounces macaroni
- 1 tablespoon salt
- 2 cups heavy cream
- 1 ¼ pounds American cheese
- 2 tablespoons Parmesan cheese
- 1 tablespoon Romano cheese
- 4 ounces Colby Jack Cheese, shredded

How to Prepare

1. In a large pan of lightly salted boiling water, cook the macaroni for about 8–10 minutes or according to package's directions.
2. Drain the macaroni well and transfer into a large bowl.
3. Preheat the oven to broiler on high.
4. In a medium-sized heavy-bottomed pan, add heavy cream, American cheese, Parmesan cheese, and Romano cheese over medium heat and cook for about 2–3 minutes or until cheeses are melted, stirring frequently.
5. In the bottom of a 9 x 13-inch baking dish, place the cooked pasta and top with cream mixture.
6. Sprinkle with Colby Jack cheese and broil for about 3–5 minutes or until top becomes golden-brown.
7. Serve hot.

Preparation time: 15 minutes
Cooking time: 18 minutes
Total time: 33 minutes
Servings: 8

Nutritional Values

- ➢ *Calories 611*
- ➢ *Total Fat 34.9 g*
- ➢ *Saturated Fat 21 g*
- ➢ *Cholesterol 112 mg*
- ➢ *Sodium 1,900 mg*
- ➢ *Total Carbs 49.3 g*
- ➢ *Fiber 1.8 g*
- ➢ *Sugar 6.8 g*
- ➢ *Protein 24.8 g*

"Chili's" Cajun Chicken Pasta

Ingredients

- ➤ 8 ounces penne pasta
- ➤ 2 boneless skinless chicken breasts
- ➤ 4 teaspoons Cajun seasoning
- ➤ 4 tablespoons butter, divided
- ➤ 3 cups half-and-half
- ➤ ½ teaspoon lemon pepper seasoning
- ➤ 1 teaspoon salt
- ➤ 1 teaspoon ground black pepper

- ➢ ¼ teaspoon garlic powder
- ➢ 2 tomatoes, chopped
- ➢ ½ cup Parmesan cheese, shredded

How to Prepare

1. In a large pan of lightly salted boiling water, cook the pasta for about 8–10 minutes or according to package's directions.
2. Drain the pasta well and transfer into a large bowl.
3. Meanwhile, in a bowl, place chicken breasts and Cajun seasoning and toss to coat well.
4. In a large wok, melt 2 tablespoons of butter over medium and sear the chicken breasts for about 10–12 minutes or until cooked through, flipping occasionally.
5. Remove the chicken breasts from heat and place onto a cutting board.
6. Cut the chicken breasts into strips.
7. In a frying pan, add remaining butter, half-and-half, lemon pepper, salt, pepper, and garlic powder over medium heat and cook for about 2–3 minutes, stirring occasionally.
8. Remove from heat and pour the sauce over pasta.
9. Stir the pasta with sauce and divide onto serving plates.
10. Top each plate with chicken strips, followed by tomatoes and Parmesan cheese.
11. Serve immediately.

Preparation time: 15 minutes
Cooking time: 15 minutes
Total time: 30 minutes
Servings: 4

Nutritional Values

- ➢ *Calories 716*
- ➢ *Total Fat 42.9 g*
- ➢ *Saturated Fat 24 g*
- ➢ *Cholesterol 222 mg*

- ➢ *Sodium 900 mg*
- ➢ *Total Carbs 41.9 g*
- ➢ *Fiber 0.8 g*
- ➢ *Sugar 2 g*
- ➢ *Protein 40.9 g*

"The Cheesecake Factory" Four Cheese Pasta

Ingredients

- ➢ 1 (16-ounce) package ziti pasta
- ➢ 2 (10-ounce) cartons refrigerated Alfredo sauce
- ➢ 1 cup sour cream
- ➢ 2 large eggs, lightly beaten
- ➢ 1 (15-ounce) carton ricotta cheese
- ➢ ½ cup Parmesan cheese, grated and divided

➢ ¼ cup Romano cheese, grated
➢ ¼ cup fresh parsley, minced
➢ 1 ¾ cups part-skim mozzarella cheese, shredded

How to Prepare

1. Preheat the oven to 350°F.
2. Lightly, grease a baking dish.
3. In a large pan of lightly salted boiling water, cook the pasta for about 8–10 minutes or until according to package's directions.
4. Drain the pasta completely and return to the same pan.
5. In the pan with pasta, add the Alfredo sauce and sour cream and stir to combine.
6. In a small bowl, add the eggs, ricotta cheese, ¼ cup of Parmesan cheese, Romano cheese and parsley and mix well.
7. In the bottom of prepared baking dish, place half of the pasta mixture and top with cheese mixture, followed by the remaining pasta mixture
8. Sprinkle with mozzarella cheese, followed by the remaining Parmesan.
9. Cover the baking dish and bake for about 25 minutes.
10. Uncover the baking dish and bake for about 5–10 minutes or until bubbly.

Preparation time: 15 minutes
Cooking time: 45 minutes
Total time: 1 hour
Servings: 8

Nutritional Values

➢ *Calories 699*
➢ *Total Fat 31.7 g*
➢ *Saturated Fat 18.4 g*
➢ *Cholesterol 163 mg*
➢ *Sodium 2,020 mg*

> *Total Carbs 70.1 g*
> *Fiber 0.1 g*
> *Sugar 0.3 g*
> *Protein 34.2 g*

"Olive Garden" Capellini Primavera

Ingredients

- ➢ 4 ounces butter
- ➢ 5 cups broccoli, cut into 1-inch pieces
- ➢ 1 ½ cups onions, chopped
- ➢ ¾ cup carrots, peeled and julienned
- ➢ 3 cups fresh mushrooms, sliced
- ➢ 1 ¼ cups yellow squash, halved lengthwise and sliced thinly

- ➢ 1 teaspoon vegetable broth
- ➢ ¼ cup oil-packed sun-dried tomatoes, minced
- ➢ 1 ¼ cups canned crushed tomatoes with juice
- ➢ 1 tablespoon fresh parsley, chopped finely
- ➢ ¼ teaspoon dried oregano
- ➢ ¼ teaspoon dried rosemary
- ➢ 1/8 teaspoon red pepper flakes, crushed
- ➢ 1 pound cooked hot angel-hair pasta
- ➢ ½ cup Parmesan cheese, grated

How to Prepare

1. In a Dutch oven, melt the butter oven over medium heat and sauté the broccoli, onions, and carrots for about 5 minutes.
2. Add the mushrooms, squash, and garlic, and sauté for about 2 minutes.
3. Stir in the remaining ingredients except for pasta and cheese and bring to a gentle boil.
4. Simmer for about 8–10 minutes.
5. Divide the pasta onto serving plates and top with veggie mixture.
6. Serve with the garnishing of Parmesan cheese.

Preparation time: 20 minutes
Cooking time: 20 minutes
Total time: 40 minutes
Servings: 5

Nutritional Values

- ➢ *Calories 528*
- ➢ *Total Fat 23.1 g*
- ➢ *Saturated Fat 12.9 g*
- ➢ *Cholesterol 121 mg*
- ➢ *Sodium 308 mg*
- ➢ *Total Carbs 65.2 g*
- ➢ *Fiber 4.9 g*

➤ *Sugar 5.3 g*
➤ *Protein 18.9 g*

"The Cheesecake Factory" Bristo Shrimp Pasta

Ingredients

- ➢ 4 ounces uncooked angel hair pasta
- ➢ ¼ cup olive oil
- ➢ 8 jumbo shrimp, peeled and deveined

- ➤ 6 fresh asparagus spears, trimmed and cut into 2-inch pieces
- ➤ 2 garlic cloves, minced
- ➤ ½ cup fresh mushrooms, sliced
- ➤ 1 small plum tomato; peeled, seeded, and chopped
- ➤ Salt, to taste
- ➤ ½ cup chicken broth
- ➤ 1/8 teaspoon red pepper flakes, crushed
- ➤ 1 tablespoon fresh basil, minced
- ➤ 1 tablespoon oregano, minced
- ➤ 1 tablespoon thyme, minced
- ➤ 1 tablespoon parsley, minced
- ➤ ¼ cup Parmesan cheese, grated

How to Prepare

1. In a large pan of lightly salted boiling water, cook the pasta for about 8–10 minutes or until according to package's directions.
2. Drain the pasta completely.
3. Meanwhile, in a large wok, heat the oil over medium heat and cook the shrimp and asparagus for about 3–4 minutes.
4. Add the garlic and cook for about 1 minute.
5. Add the mushrooms, tomato, pepper flakes and broth and simmer for about 2 minutes.
6. Add the pasta and herbs and toss to coat.
7. Serve hot with the sprinkling of cheese.

Preparation time: 15 minutes
Cooking time: 10 minutes
Total time: 25 minutes
Servings: 2

Nutritional Values

- ➤ *Calories 648*
- ➤ *Total Fat 36.9 g*
- ➤ *Saturated Fat 9.5 g*

- ➢ *Cholesterol 257 mg*
- ➢ *Sodium 1,202 mg*
- ➢ *Total Carbs 41.5 g*
- ➢ *Fiber 3.3 g*
- ➢ *Sugar 2 g*
- ➢ *Protein 42.5g*

"Red Lobster" Crab Alfredo

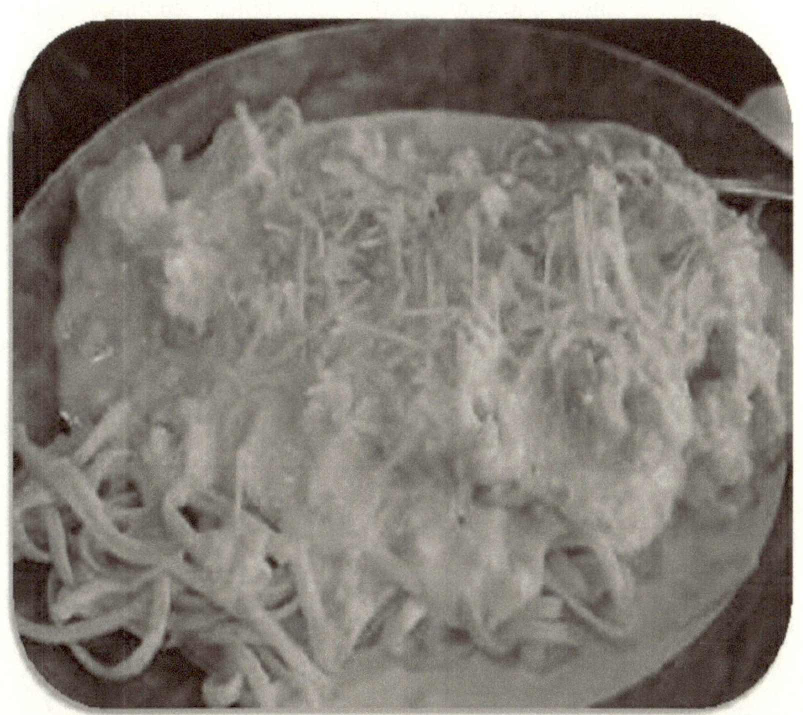

Ingredients

- 16 ounces linguini pasta
- 4 ounces unsalted butter
- 2 tablespoons cream cheese
- 2 cups half-and-half
- ¾ cup Parmesan cheese, shredded
- 1 teaspoon garlic powder
- Salt and ground black pepper, to taste

➢ 8 ounces crab lump meat

How to Prepare

1. **Sauce:** In a saucepan, melt butter over medium-low heat and stir in cream cheese until softened.
2. Add half-and-half and the Parmesan cheese and stir to combine.
3. Add garlic powder, salt, and black pepper, and stir to combine.
4. Reduce the heat to low and simmer for about 15–20 minutes, stirring occasionally.
5. Meanwhile, in a large pan of salted boiling water, add crab legs over medium heat and cook for about 6 minutes.
6. With a slotted spoon, remove the crab legs from the water and transfer into a large bowl.
7. With a cracker, remove the meat from the crab legs.
8. Meanwhile, in a large pan of lightly salted boiling water, add pasta and cook for about 8–10 minutes or according to package's instructions.
9. Drain the pasta and transfer into a large bowl.
10. Add sauce and stir to combine well.
11. Add crab meat and gently stir to combine.
12. Serve immediately.

Preparation time: 20 minutes
Cooking time: 20 minutes
Total time: 40 minutes
Servings: 6

Nutritional Values

➢ *Calories 557*
➢ *Total Fat 34.3 g*
➢ *Saturated Fat 18 g*
➢ *Cholesterol 103 mg*
➢ *Sodium 569 mg*
➢ *Total Carbs 52.1 g*

➢ *Fiber 3.4 g*
➢ *Sugar 0.3 g*
➢ *Protein 17.6 g*

CHAPTER 10
DESSERT RECIPES

"Baskin-Robbins" Chocolate Ice Cream

Ingredients

- ¾ cup sugar, divided
- 4 egg yolks
- 2 cups bittersweet chocolate baking chips, melted and cooled

- ➢ 2 ½ teaspoons instant coffee granules
- ➢ 1 ½ cups milk
- ➢ 1 ½ cups heavy whipping cream
- ➢ 1 teaspoon vanilla extract
- ➢ ¾ cup semisweet chocolate chips, melted
- ➢ ¾ cup slivered almonds, toasted
- ➢ 1/3 cup milk chocolate toffee bits

How to Prepare

1. In a small bowl, add egg yolks and ¼ cup of sugar and beat until well combined.
2. Stir in bittersweet chocolate chips and coffee granules. Set aside.
3. In a large saucepan, add milk over medium-low heat and cook until heated.
4. Add the remaining sugar and stir until dissolved.
5. In the bowl of egg yolk mixture, add small amount of hot milk mixture and beat well.
6. Immediately, return the mixture into the pan, beating continuously.
7. Reduce the heat to low and cook for about 2–3 minutes or mixture becomes thick enough to coat a metal spoon, stirring continuously.
8. Immediately, remove the pan from heat and transfer the mixture into a large bowl.
9. Place the bowl in a pan of ice water for about 2 minutes, stirring gently and occasionally.
10. Remove the bowl from ice bath and stir in cream and vanilla extract.
11. Arrange a plastic wrap on top of custard and press on the surface.
12. Refrigerate overnight.
13. Place melted semisweet chocolate onto a wax paper-lined baking sheet and with a spoon, spread into 1/8-inch thickness.
14. Refrigerate for about 20 minutes.
15. Remove from refrigerator and chop the chocolate roughly.
16. Place the custard into an ice cream in 2 batches and process

according to manufacturer's directions.

17. Transfer ice cream into freezer containers and stir in chopped chocolate, almonds, and toffee bits.

18. Freeze for about 2–4 hours or until set before serving.

Preparation time: 20 minutes
Cooking time: 10 minutes
Total time: 30 minutes
Servings: 8

Nutritional Values

➤ *Calories 634*
➤ *Total Fat 37.8 g*
➤ *Saturated Fat 21 g*
➤ *Cholesterol 151 mg*
➤ *Sodium 102 mg*
➤ *Total Carbs 68.4 g*
➤ *Fiber 3.7 g*
➤ *Sugar 59.5 g*
➤ *Protein 8.4 g*

"Wendy's" Chocolate Frosty

Ingredients

- ➤ 1 cup heavy whipping cream
- ➤ 1 tablespoon almond butter
- ➤ 2 tablespoons cacao powder
- ➤ ½ teaspoon liquid stevia
- ➤ 1 teaspoon vanilla extract

How to Prepare

1. In the bowl of a stand mixer, add all ingredients and beat until stiff peaks form.
2. Freeze the mixture for about 30–60 minutes until barely frozen.
3. Place the frosty in a plastic freezer bag.
4. Cut one corner, and pipe into serving cups.
5. Serve immediately.

Preparation time: 15 minutes
Total time: 15 minutes
Servings: 4

Nutritional Values

- *Calories 137*
- *Total Fat 13.9 g*
- *Saturated Fat 7.4 g*
- *Cholesterol 41 mg*
- *Sodium 12 mg*
- *Total Carbs 3 g*
- *Fiber 1.2 g*
- *Sugar 0.3 g*
- *Protein 2 g*

"Culver's" Frozen Custard

Ingredients

- ➢ 1 ½ cups sugar
- ➢ ¼ cup all-purpose flour
- ➢ ½ teaspoon salt
- ➢ 4 cups whole milk
- ➢ 4 large eggs, lightly beaten
- ➢ 4 cups heavy whipping cream
- ➢ 3 tablespoons vanilla extract

How to Prepare

1. In a large heavy saucepan, add sugar, flour, and salt, and mix well.
2. Slowly, add milk, beating continuously until smooth.
3. Place saucepan over medium heat and cook until thickened and bubbly, stirring continuously.
4. Reduce the heat to low and cook for about 2 minutes, stirring continuously.
5. Remove the saucepan from heat and set aside.
6. In a small bowl, add a small amount of hot milk mixture and eggs and mix well.
7. Immediately, return the mixture into the pan and bring to a gentle simmer, beating continuously.
8. Cook for about 2 minutes, stirring continuously.
9. Immediately, remove the pan from heat and transfer the mixture into a large bowl.
10. Place the bowl in a pan of ice water for about 2 minutes, stirring gently and occasionally.
11. Remove the bowl from ice bath.
12. Arrange a plastic wrap on top of custard and press on the surface.
13. Refrigerate overnight.
14. Place the custard into an ice cream in 2 batches and process according to manufacturer's directions.
15. Transfer ice cream into freezer containers and freeze for about 2–4 hours or until set before serving.

Preparation time: 15 minutes
Cooking time: 5 minutes
Total time: 20 minutes
Servings: 8

Nutritional Values

➤ *Calories 485*
➤ *Total Fat 28.7 g*

- ➢ *Saturated Fat 16.9 g*
- ➢ *Cholesterol 187 mg*
- ➢ *Sodium 254 mg*
- ➢ *Total Carbs 48.5 g*
- ➢ *Fiber 0.1 g*
- ➢ *Sugar 44.8 g*
- ➢ *Protein 8.7 g*

"Starbucks" Cranberry Bliss Bars

Ingredients

<u>Bars</u>

- ➢ 2 ¼ cups all-purpose flour
- ➢ 1 ½ teaspoons baking powder
- ➢ 1/8 teaspoon ground cinnamon
- ➢ ¼ teaspoon salt
- ➢ ¾ cup melted hot butter
- ➢ 1 ½ cups light brown sugar

- ➤ 2 large eggs, room temperature
- ➤ ¾ teaspoon vanilla extract
- ➤ ½ cup dried cranberries
- ➤ 6 ounces white baking chocolate, chopped roughly

Frosting

- ➤ 1 (8-ounce) package cream cheese, softened
- ➤ 1 cup confectioners' sugar
- ➤ 1 tablespoon orange zest, grated
- ➤ 6 ounces white baking chocolate, melted
- ➤ ½ cup dried cranberries, chopped

How to Prepare

1. Preheat the oven to 350°F.
2. Grease a 13 x 9-inch baking dish.
3. **Bars:** In a bowl, add flour, baking powder, cinnamon, and salt, and mix well.
4. In a separate bowl, add hot melted butter and brown sugar and mix well.
5. Set aside to cool slightly.
6. After cooling, add eggs, 1 at a time, beating well after each addition.
7. Add vanilla extract and mix well.
8. Add flour mixture and mix until just combined.
9. Fold in cranberries and chocolate.
10. Place the mixture into the prepared baking dish and with the back of a spoon, smooth the top surface.
11. Bake for about 18–21 minutes.
12. Remove the baking dish from oven and place onto a wire rack to cool completely.
13. **Frosting:** In a bowl, add cream cheese, confectioners' sugar, and orange zest, and beat until smooth.
14. Add half of white chocolate and beat until well combined.
15. Spread the frosting over cooled bars and sprinkle with cranberries.

16. Drizzle with remaining melted chocolate.

17. Cut into triangles and serve.

Preparation time: 20 minutes
Cooking time: 21 minutes
Total time: 41 minutes
Servings: 12

Nutritional Values

- *Calories 541*
- *Total Fat 27.3 g*
- *Saturated Fat 17.8 g*
- *Cholesterol 82 mg*
- *Sodium 226 mg*
- *Total Carbs 71 g*
- *Fiber 1.2 g*
- *Sugar 51.2 g*
- *Protein 7.1 g*

"McDonald's" Fried Apple Pie

Ingredients

<u>Crust</u>

- ➢ 1 (8-ounce) package cream cheese, softened
- ➢ 1 cup unsalted butter, softened
- ➢ 2 cups all-purpose flour
- ➢ ¼ teaspoon salt

<u>Filling</u>

- ➢ ¼ cup sugar
- ➢ ¼ teaspoon ground cinnamon
- ➢ 1/8 teaspoon ground allspice
- ➢ 2 cups tart apples; peeled, cored, and chopped finely
- ➢ 2 tablespoons cold unsalted butter

Egg Wash

- ➢ 1 large egg yolk
- ➢ 2 tablespoons water

Topping

- ➢ 2 tablespoons coarse sugar
- ➢ 2 tablespoons cinnamon-sugar

How to Prepare

1. **Crust:** In a bowl, mix together flour and salt.
2. In a separate large bowl, add cream cheese and butter and beat until smooth.
3. Slowly, add flour mixture and beat until well combined.
4. Divide the dough into 2 balls and then, press each into a disk.
5. With a plastic wrap, cover each dough disk and refrigerate for 1 hour.
6. Preheat the oven to 425°F.
7. **Filling:** In a bowl, mix together sugar, cinnamon, and allspice. Set aside.
8. Divide each dough disk into 12 balls.
9. Place each dough ball onto a lightly floured surface and then, roll each into a 4-inch circle.
10. Arrange the dough circles onto a smooth surface.
11. Place about 1 tablespoon of chopped apples on one side of each dough circle and sprinkle with ½ teaspoon of sugar mixture.
12. Place about ¼ teaspoon of butter on top of each in the form of dot.
13. In a small bowl, beat together egg yolk and water.
14. Brush the edges of each pastry with egg wash and then fold it over

the filling.

15. With a fork, seal edges firmly.
16. Arrange the pastries lace onto 2 ungreased baking sheets about 2 inches apart.
17. Brush the top of each pastry with remaining egg wash.
18. With a knife, cut a slit in the top of each pastry and sprinkle with coarse sugar and cinnamon-sugar.
19. Bake for about 11–14 minutes, or until golden-brown.
20. Remove the baking sheets from oven and place onto wire racks to cool before serving.

Preparation time: 25 minutes
Cooking time: 14 minutes
Total time: 39 minutes
Servings: 12

Nutritional Values

- *Calories 335*
- *Total Fat 24.5 g*
- *Saturated Fat 15.3 g*
- *Cholesterol 84 mg*
- *Sodium 240 mg*
- *Total Carbs 25.8 g*
- *Fiber 1.5 g*
- *Sugar 8.2 g*
- *Protein 4.1 g*

"Olive Garden" Zabaglione

Ingredients

- ➤ ½ cup fresh strawberries, hulled and sliced
- ➤ 3 tablespoons plus 1 teaspoon white sugar, divided
- ➤ ¼ cup dry Marsala wine
- ➤ 3 large egg yolks

How to Prepare

1. In a bowl, add the strawberries and 1 teaspoon of sugar and gently toss to coat.
2. Cover the bowl and set aside at room temperature for about 1 hour.
3. Now, divide the strawberry slices in 2 small serving bowls.
4. In a small pan, add the wine, egg yolk and remaining sugar over low heat and cook for about 7–8 minutes, beating continuously.
5. Remove from the heat and place the custard over the strawberries.
6. Serve warm.

Preparation time: 15 minutes
Cooking time: 8 minutes
Total time: 23 minutes
Servings: 2

Nutritional Values
- *Calories 185*
- *Total Fat 6.9 g*
- *Saturated Fat 2.4 g*
- *Cholesterol 315 mg*
- *Sodium 14 mg*
- *Total Carbs 22.5 g*
- *Fiber 0.7 g*
- *Sugar 20.1 g*
- *Protein 4.3 g*

"Cracker Barrel" Baked Apple Dumplings

Ingredients

- ➤ 2 medium Granny Smith apples, peeled and cored
- ➤ 2 (8-ounce) tubes refrigerated crescent rolls
- ➤ 1 cup sugar
- ➤ 1/3 cup butter, softened
- ➤ ½ teaspoon ground cinnamon

➢ ¾ cup Mountain Dew soda
➢ Vanilla ice cream, for topping

How to Prepare

1. Preheat the oven to 350°F.
2. Grease a 13 x 9-inch baking dish.
3. Cut each apple into 8 wedges.
4. Unroll both crescent dough tubes and separate each into 8 triangles.
5. Wrap a dough triangle around each apple wedge.
6. Arrange the dumplings into the prepared baking dish in a single layer.
7. In a bowl, add sugar, butter and cinnamon and mix until well combined.
8. Sprinkle the sugar mixture over dumplings evenly.
9. Carefully, pour soda around the rolls.
10. Bake for about 35–40 minutes, or until golden-brown.
11. Serve warm with the topping of ice cream.

Preparation time: 15 minutes
Cooking time: 15 minutes
Total time: 30 minutes
Servings: 8

Nutritional Values

➢ *Calories 377*
➢ *Total Fat 11.4 g*
➢ *Saturated Fat 5.6 g*
➢ *Cholesterol 23 mg*
➢ *Sodium 363 mg*
➢ *Total Carbs 65.2 g*
➢ *Fiber 2.6 g*
➢ *Sugar 36.9 g*
➢ *Protein 6.4 g*

"Starbucks" Lemon Loaf

Ingredients

<u>Cake</u>

- ➤ 6 eggs
- ➤ 2/3 cup erythritol
- ➤ 2 tablespoons cream cheese, softened
- ➤ 1 teaspoon vanilla extract
- ➤ 2 tablespoons heavy whipping cream
- ➤ 1½ teaspoons baking powder

- ➢ ½ teaspoon salt
- ➢ 9 tablespoons butter, melted and cooled
- ➢ ½ cup plus 2 tablespoons coconut flour
- ➢ 2 teaspoons lemon zest, grated
- ➢ 4 tablespoons fresh lemon juice

Glaze
- ➢ 2 tablespoons powdered erythritol
- ➢ 2 teaspoons fresh lemon juice
- ➢ 1 teaspoon lemon zest, grated
- ➢ Splash of heavy whipping cream

How to Prepare

1. Preheat the oven to 325ºF. Line a bread pan with parchment paper.
2. **Cake:** In a bowl, add the eggs, erythritol, cream cheese, vanilla extract, heavy whipping cream, baking powder, and salt, and beat until well combined.
3. Add the remaining ingredients and beat until well combined.
4. Place the mixture into the prepared loaf pan evenly.
5. Bake for about 55–60 minutes or until a toothpick inserted in the center comes out clean.
6. Remove the bread pan from oven and place onto a wire rack to cool for about 10 minutes.
7. Now, invert the cake onto the wire rack to cool before glazing.
8. **Glaze:** In a bowl, add all the ingredients and beat until smooth.
9. Spread the glaze over the cake evenly and serve.

Preparation time: 15 minutes
Cooking time: 1 hour
Total time: 1 hour, 15 minutes
Servings: 5

Nutritional Values
- ➢ *Calories 602*

- ➤ *Total Fat 52 g*
- ➤ *Saturated Fat 3.2 g*
- ➤ *Cholesterol 440 mg*
- ➤ *Sodium 786 mg*
- ➤ *Total Carbs 20 g*
- ➤ *Fiber 10.3 g*
- ➤ *Sugar 1.5 g*
- ➤ *Protein 15.7 g*

"The Cheesecake Factory" Key Lime Cheesecake

Ingredients

Crust

- ➢ 2 cups graham cracker crumbs, crushed
- ➢ ½ cup butter, melted
- ➢ ¼ cup granulated sugar

Filling

- ➢ 3 (8-ounce) packages cream cheese, softened
- ➢ 1 cup sugar
- ➢ 1 cup sour cream
- ➢ ¼ cup flour
- ➢ 2 teaspoons vanilla extract
- ➢ 4 eggs
- ➢ ¾ cup fresh key lime juice

How to Prepare

1. Preheat the oven to 375ºF.
2. **Crust:** In a bowl, add the graham cracker crumbs and cinnamon and mix well.
3. Add butter and mix until a crumbly mixture forms.
4. Place the crumb mixture into a 10-inch springform pan and, press into an even layer onto the bottom and halfway up the sides of pan.
5. Bake for about 7–8 minutes.
6. Again, set the temperature of oven to 375ºF.
7. Meanwhile, in a bowl, add cream cheese and beat until smooth.
8. Add the sugar and beat until smooth.
9. Add the sour cream, eggs, flour, and vanilla extract, and beat until smooth.
10. Add the lime juice and stir to combine.
11. Place the filling mixture over the crust evenly.
12. Bake for about 15 minutes.
13. Now, set the temperature of oven to 250ºF and bake for about 50 minutes.
14. Remove the pan from oven and place onto a wire rack to cool for about 45–60 minutes.
15. Now, refrigerate for at least 6 hours before serving.

Preparation time: 15 minutes
Cooking time: 58 minutes
Total time: 1 hour, 13 minutes

Servings: 12

Nutritional Values

- ➤ *Calories 481*
- ➤ *Total Fat 34.3 g*
- ➤ *Saturated Fat 20.3 g*
- ➤ *Cholesterol 146 mg*
- ➤ *Sodium 378 mg*
- ➤ *Total Carbs 37.1 g*
- ➤ *Fiber 1 g*
- ➤ *Sugar 23.9 g*
- ➤ *Protein 8 g*

"The Cheesecake Factory"
Tiramisu

Ingredients

- ½ cup heavy whipping cream
- 2 cups vanilla yogurt
- 1 cup fat-free milk
- ½ cup brewed espresso, cooled
- 24 crisp ladyfinger cookies

➢ Baking cocoa, for dusting

How to Prepare

1. In a small bowl, add cream and beat until stiff peaks form.
2. Gently, fold in the yogurt.
3. In the bottom of an 8-inch square dish, place ½ cup of cream mixture evenly.
4. In a shallow dish, mix together the milk and espresso.
5. Dip 12 ladyfinger cookies into espresso mixture, allowing excess to drip off.
6. Arrange the dipped ladyfinger cookies over cream mixture in a single layer.
7. Top with half of the remaining cream mixture evenly and dust with cocoa powder.
8. Repeat the layers.
9. Cover the baking dish and refrigerate for at least 2 hours before serving.

Preparation time: 15 minutes
Total time: 15 minutes
Servings: 9

Nutritional Values
➢ *Calories 199*
➢ *Total Fat 6.3 g*
➢ *Saturated Fat 3.3 g*
➢ *Cholesterol 90 mg*
➢ *Sodium 108 mg*
➢ *Total Carbs 26.1 g*
➢ *Fiber 0.4 g*
➢ *Sugar 5.2 g*
➢ *Protein 7.8 g*

CONCLUSION

Whether you are an expert cook or have just started practicing your cooking skills, you can try all the flavorsome copycat recipes shared in this cookbook. All the recipes are designed and recreated with the sole purpose of bringing those classic restaurant-like flavors to every other household. It's about time that you put on your apron and surprise your friends and family with authentic restaurant flavors!